PRACTICE - ASSESS - DIAGNOSE

180 Days of WRITING for Fourth Grade

Author
Kristin Kemp, M.A.Ed.

Standards

For information on how this resource meets national and other state standards, see pages 4–6; 13. You may also review this information by scanning the QR code or visiting our website at http://www.shelleducation.com and following the on-screen directions.

Publishing Credits

Corinne Burton, M.A.Ed., *President*; Emily R. Smith, M.A.Ed., *Content Director*; Jennifer Wilson, *Editor*; Grace Alba Le, *Multimedia Designer*; Don Tran, *Production Artist*; Stephanie Bernard, *Assistant Editor*; Amber Goff, *Editorial Assistant*

Image Credits

pp. 26, 34, 35, 37, 46, 47, 51, 52, 63, 64, 72, 84, 87, 89, 102, 119, 128, 153, 165, 193, iStock; All other images Shutterstock.

Standards

Shell Education
5482 Argosy Avenue
Huntington Beach, CA 92649-1030
www.tcmpub.com/shell-education

ISBN: 978-1-4258-1527-1

TABLE OF CONTENTS

INTRODUCTION

The Need for Practice

To be successful in today's writing classrooms, students must deeply understand both concepts and procedures so that they can discuss and demonstrate their understanding. Demonstrating understanding is a process that must be continually practiced for students to be successful. Practice is especially important to help students apply their concrete, conceptual understanding of each particular writing skill.

Understanding Assessment

In addition to providing opportunities for frequent practice, teachers must be able to assess students' writing skills. This is important so that teachers can adequately address students' misconceptions, build on their current understandings, and challenge them appropriately. Assessment is a long-term process that involves careful analysis of student responses from a discussion, project, practice sheet, or test. When analyzing the data, it is important for teachers to reflect on how their teaching practices may have influenced students' responses and to identify those areas where additional instruction may be required. In short, the data gathered from assessments should be used to inform instruction: slow down, speed up, or reteach. This type of assessment is called *formative assessment.*

HOW TO USE THIS BOOK

With *180 Days of Writing*, creative, theme-based units guide students as they practice the five steps of the writing process: prewriting, drafting, revising, editing, and publishing. During each odd week (Weeks 1, 3, 5, etc.), students interact with mentor texts. Then, students apply their learning by writing their own pieces during each following even week (Weeks 2, 4, 6, etc.). Many practice pages also focus on grammar/language standards to help improve students' writing.

Easy to Use and Standards Based

These daily activities reinforce grade-level skills across the various genres of writing: opinion, informative/explanatory, and narrative. Each day provides a full practice page, making the activities easy to prepare and implement as part of a classroom morning routine, at the beginning of each writing lesson, or as homework.

The chart below indicates the writing and language standards that are addressed throughout this book. See pages 5–6 for a breakdown of which writing standard is covered in each week. **Note:** Students may not have deep understandings of some topics in this book. Remember to assess students based on their writing skills and not their content knowledge.

College and Career Readiness Standards

Writing 4.1—Write opinion pieces on topics or texts, supporting a point of view with reasons and information.
Writing 4.2—Write informative/explanatory texts to examine a topic and convey ideas and information clearly.
Writing 4.3—Write narratives to develop real or imagined experiences or events using effective technique, descriptive details, and clear event sequences.
Language 4.1—Demonstrate command of the conventions of standard English grammar and usage when writing or speaking.
Language 4.2—Demonstrate command of the conventions of standard English capitalization, punctuation, and spelling when writing.
Language 4.3—Use knowledge of language and its conventions when writing, speaking, reading, or listening.
Language 4.4—Determine or clarify the meaning of unknown and multiple-meaning words and phrases based on *grade 4 reading and content*, choosing flexibly from a range of strategies.
Language 4.5—Demonstrate understanding of figurative language, word relationships, and nuances in word meanings.

HOW TO USE THIS BOOK *(cont.)*

Below is a list of overarching themes, corresponding weekly themes, and the writing standards that students will encounter throughout this book. For each overarching theme, students will interact with mentor texts in the odd week and then apply their learning by writing their own pieces in the even week. **Note:** The writing prompt for each week can be found on pages 7–8. You may wish to display the prompts in the classroom for students to reference throughout the appropriate weeks.

Overarching Themes	Weekly Themes	Standards
Ancient Egypt	**Week 1:** Hieroglyphics **Week 2:** Pyramids	**Writing 4.2**—Write informative/explanatory texts to examine a topic and convey ideas and information clearly.
International Sports	**Week 3:** Hurling **Week 4:** Cricket	**Writing 4.1**—Write opinion pieces on topics or texts, supporting a point of view with reasons and information.
Dessert	**Week 5:** Cupcakes **Week 6:** Ice Cream	**Writing 4.3**—Write narratives to develop real or imagined experiences or events using effective technique, descriptive details, and clear event sequences.
Human Body	**Week 7:** Skeleton **Week 8:** Muscles	**Writing 4.2**—Write informative/explanatory texts to examine a topic and convey ideas and information clearly.
Communication	**Week 9:** Morse Code **Week 10:** Telegrams	**Writing 4.1**—Write opinion pieces on topics or texts, supporting a point of view with reasons and information.
Dog Breeds	**Week 11:** Great Danes **Week 12:** Chihuahuas	**Writing 4.2**—Write informative/explanatory texts to examine a topic and convey ideas and information clearly.
National Parks	**Week 13:** Yosemite **Week 14:** Grand Canyon	**Writing 4.3**—Write narratives to develop real or imagined experiences or events using effective technique, descriptive details, and clear event sequences.
Recess Games	**Week 15:** Four Square **Week 16:** Kickball	**Writing 4.3**—Write narratives to develop real or imagined experiences or events using effective technique, descriptive details, and clear event sequences.
Transportation Innovators	**Week 17:** The Wright Brothers **Week 18:** Henry Ford	**Writing 4.2**—Write informative/explanatory texts to examine a topic and convey ideas and information clearly.

HOW TO USE THIS BOOK *(cont.)*

Overarching Themes	Weekly Themes	Standards
Winter Sports	**Week 19:** Snowboarding **Week 20:** Ice Skating	**Writing 4.3**—Write narratives to develop real or imagined experiences or events using effective technique, descriptive details, and clear event sequences.
Composers	**Week 21:** Mozart **Week 22:** Beethoven	**Writing 4.1**—Write opinion pieces on topics or texts, supporting a point of view with reasons and information.
Space	**Week 23:** Asteroids **Week 24:** Comets	**Writing 4.2**—Write informative/explanatory texts to examine a topic and convey ideas and information clearly.
Clean Energy	**Week 25:** Solar Energy **Week 26:** Turbines	**Writing 4.1**—Write opinion pieces on topics or texts, supporting a point of view with reasons and information.
Mountain Peaks	**Week 27:** Mount Everest **Week 28:** Mount Kilimanjaro	**Writing 4.1**—Write opinion pieces on topics or texts, supporting a point of view with reasons and information.
Art	**Week 29:** Sculpture **Week 30:** Painting	**Writing 4.2**—Write informative/explanatory texts to examine a topic and convey ideas and information clearly.
Trains	**Week 31:** Steam Engine Trains **Week 32:** Bullet Trains	**Writing 4.1**—Write opinion pieces on topics or texts, supporting a point of view with reasons and information.
European Monuments	**Week 33:** Eiffel Tower **Week 34:** Leaning Tower of Pisa	**Writing 4.3**—Write narratives to develop real or imagined experiences or events using effective technique, descriptive details, and clear event sequences.
Summer Fun	**Week 35:** Camping **Week 36:** Swimming	**Writing 4.3**—Write narratives to develop real or imagined experiences or events using effective technique, descriptive details, and clear event sequences.

HOW TO USE THIS BOOK *(cont.)*

Weekly Setup

Write each prompt on the board throughout the appropriate week. Students should reference the prompts as they work through the activity pages so that they stay focused on the topics and the right genre of writing: opinion, informative/explanatory, and narrative. You may wish to print copies of this chart from the digital resources (filename: G4_writingprompts.pdf) and distribute them to students to keep throughout the school year.

Week	Prompt
1	Describe what Egyptian hieroglyphics are. Include what they look like and how they are created.
2	Explain why pyramids in Egypt were built. Include what can be found in pyramids and what they are made of.
3	There are many aspects to the sport hurling. Explain your opinions on the rules and the players involved in the sport.
4	There are many aspects to the sport cricket. Explain your opinions on the rules and the players involved in the sport.
5	Describe a time when you ate a cupcake. Include what the cupcake looked like and how it felt, tasted, and smelled.
6	Describe a time you were eating an ice cream cone. Include what the ice cream looked like and how it felt, tasted, and smelled.
7	Describe the human skeleton. Include details about some of a skeleton's bones and what their functions are.
8	Explain what human muscles are. Include some types of muscles and their functions?
9	Do you think Morse code is useful? Explain why or why not. Include benefits and disadvantages to support your opinion.
10	Would you rather receive a telegram or an email? Explain why you would want to receive one over the other.

Week	Prompt
11	Write a paragraph about Great Danes. Include specific facts about the breed, including their physical characteristics, breed history, and personality.
12	Write a paragraph about Chihuahuas. Include specific facts about the breed, including their physical characteristics, breed history, and personality.
13	Imagine someone is hiking in Yosemite. Describe the experience, including details about how the person feels and what the scenery looks like.
14	Imagine you are taking a tour of the Grand Canyon on horseback. Describe the experience, including details about how you feel and what the scenery looks like.
15	Write about a time when you played four square. Describe the experience, including details about whom you played with and how the game went.
16	Write about a time when you played kickball. Describe the experience, including details about whom you played with and how the game went.
17	Write about the Wright Brothers' first flight. Include facts about where and when the flight took place.
18	Write about the production of Henry Ford's Model-T car. Include facts about the Model-T and the employees who helped make the cars.

HOW TO USE THIS BOOK *(cont.)*

Week	Prompt
19	Describe a time when someone goes snowboarding for the first time. Include details of the experience and how the character feels.
20	Describe a time when a fourth grader goes ice skating for the first time. Include details of the experience and how the character feels.
21	Should Mozart have been required to perform for royalty? Explain why you feel the way that you do. Include advantages and disadvantages to support your opinion.
22	Should Beethoven's classical music still be taught today? Explain why you think Beethoven's music should or should not be taught today.
23	Write about what an asteroid looks like. Include facts that tell about the parts of an asteroid.
24	Write about what a comet looks like. Include facts that tell about the parts of a comet.
25	Do you think solar energy is a good thing or a bad thing? Write your opinion and why you feel the way you do. Include advantages and disadvantages to support your opinion.
26	Do you think turbines should be used to collect wind energy? Write your opinion and why you feel the way you do.
27	Do you think people younger than 18 should be allowed to climb Mount Everest? Explain your opinion. Include facts that support your opinion.
28	Would you climb Mount Kilimanjaro? Explain the reasons for why you would or would not climb Mount Kilimanjaro.

Week	Prompt
29	Describe what ice sculptures are. Include details that explain how ice sculptures are created.
30	Describe what abstract art is. Include facts about what abstract art looks like.
31	Do you think steam engine trains are a good thing or a bad thing? Explain your opinion and why you feel the way you do.
32	Should the United States construct its own bullet trains? Explain your opinion and why you feel the way you do.
33	Imagine a time when a student visits the Eiffel Tower. Include details that describe how the student felt and what he or she saw.
34	Imagine a time when a student visits the Leaning Tower of Pisa. Include details that describe how the student felt and what he or she saw.
35	Imagine a time you went camping. Describe the experience, including what you did and whom you went camping with.
36	Imagine a time you went swimming. Describe the experience, including where you swam and whom you swam with.

HOW TO USE THIS BOOK *(cont.)*

Using the Practice Pages

The activity pages provide practice and assessment opportunities for each day of the school year. Teachers may wish to prepare packets of weekly practice pages for the classroom or for homework. As outlined on pages 5–6, each two-week unit is aligned to one writing standard. **Note:** Before implementing each week's activity pages, review the corresponding prompt on pages 7–8 with students and have students brainstorm thoughts about each topic.

On odd weeks, students practice the daily skills using mentor texts. On even weeks, students use what they have learned in the previous week and apply it to their own writing.

Each day focuses on one of the steps in the writing process: prewriting, drafting, revising, editing, and publishing.

There are 18 overarching themes. Each odd week and the following even week focus on unique themes that fit under one overarching theme. For a list of the overarching themes and individual weekly themes, see pages 5–6.

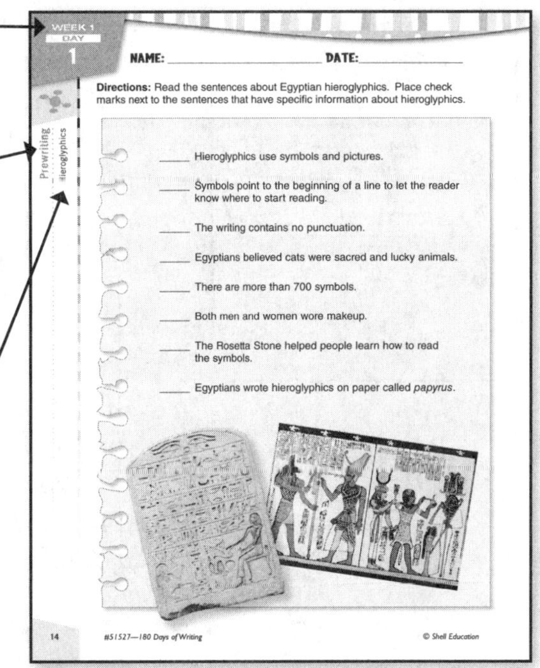

WEEK 1 DAY 1

Prewriting — Hieroglyphics

NAME: ____________ DATE: ____________

Directions: Read the sentences about Egyptian hieroglyphics. Place check marks next to the sentences that have specific information about hieroglyphics.

____ Hieroglyphics use symbols and pictures.

____ Symbols point to the beginning of a line to let the reader know where to start reading.

____ The writing contains no punctuation.

____ Egyptians believed cats were sacred and lucky animals.

____ There are more than 700 symbols.

____ Both men and women wore makeup.

____ The Rosetta Stone helped people learn how to read the symbols.

____ Egyptians wrote hieroglyphics on paper called *papyrus*.

14 #51527—180 Days of Writing © Shell Education

Using the Resources

The following resources will be helpful to students as they complete the activity pages. Print copies of these resources and provide them to students to keep at their desks.

Rubrics for the three genres of writing (opinion, informative/explanatory, and narrative) can be found on pages 202–204. Use the rubrics to assess students' writing at the end of each even week. Be sure to share these rubrics with students often so that they know what is expected of them.

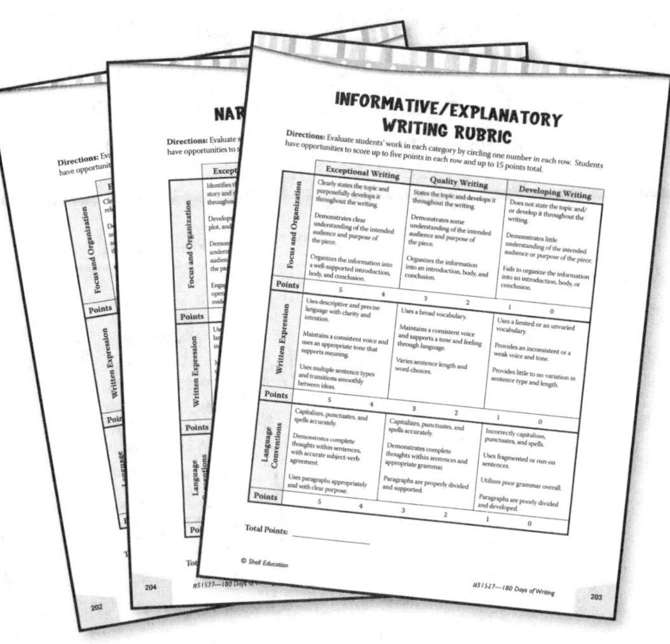

INFORMATIVE/EXPLANATORY WRITING RUBRIC

Directions: Evaluate students' work in each category by circling one number in each row. Students have opportunities to score up to five points in each row and up to 15 points total.

	Exceptional Writing	Quality Writing	Developing Writing
Focus and Organization	Clearly states the topic and purposefully develops it throughout the writing. Demonstrates clear understanding of the intended audience and purpose of the piece. Organizes the information into a well-supported introduction, body, and conclusion.	States the topic and develops it throughout the writing. Demonstrates some understanding of the intended audience and purpose of the piece. Organizes the information into an introduction, body, and conclusion.	Does not state the topic and/or develop it throughout the writing. Demonstrates little understanding of the intended audience or purpose of the piece. Fails to organize the information into an introduction, body, or conclusion.
Points	5 4	3 2	1 0
Written Expression	Uses descriptive and precise language with clarity and intention. Maintains a consistent voice and uses an appropriate tone that supports meaning. Uses multiple sentence types and transitions smoothly between ideas.	Uses a broad vocabulary. Maintains a consistent voice and supports a tone and feeling through language. Varies sentence length and word choices.	Uses a limited or an unvaried vocabulary. Provides an inconsistent or a weak voice and tone. Provides little to no variation in sentence type and length.
Points	5 4	3 2	1 0
Language Conventions	Capitalizes, punctuates, and spells accurately. Demonstrates complete thoughts within sentences, with accurate subject-verb agreement. Uses paragraphs appropriately and with clear purpose.	Capitalizes, punctuates, and spells accurately. Demonstrates complete thoughts within sentences and appropriate grammar. Paragraphs are properly divided and supported.	Incorrectly capitalizes, punctuates, and spells. Uses fragmented or run-on sentences. Utilizes poor grammar overall. Paragraphs are poorly divided and developed.
Points	5 4	3 2	1 0

Total Points: ____________

© Shell Education #51527—180 Days of Writing 203

HOW TO USE THIS BOOK *(cont.)*

Using the Resources *(cont.)*

The Writing Process can be found on page 208 and in the digital resources (filename: G4_writing_process.pdf). Students can reference each step of the writing process as they move through each week.

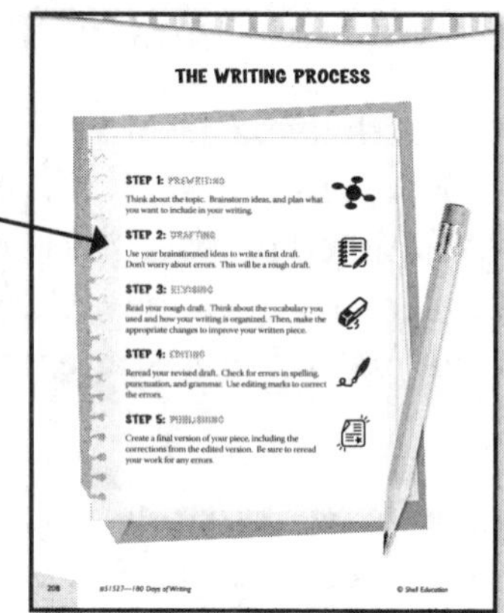

THE WRITING PROCESS

STEP 1: PREWRITING

Think about the topic. Brainstorm ideas, and plan what you want to include in your writing.

STEP 2: DRAFTING

Use your brainstormed ideas to write a first draft. Don't worry about errors. This will be a rough draft.

STEP 3: REVISING

Read your rough draft. Think about the vocabulary you used and how your writing is organized. Then, make the appropriate changes to improve your written piece.

STEP 4: EDITING

Reread your revised draft. Check for errors in spelling, punctuation, and grammar. Use editing marks to correct the errors.

STEP 5: PUBLISHING

Create a final version of your piece, including the corrections from the edited version. Be sure to reread your work for any errors.

208 #51527—180 Days of Writing © Shell Education

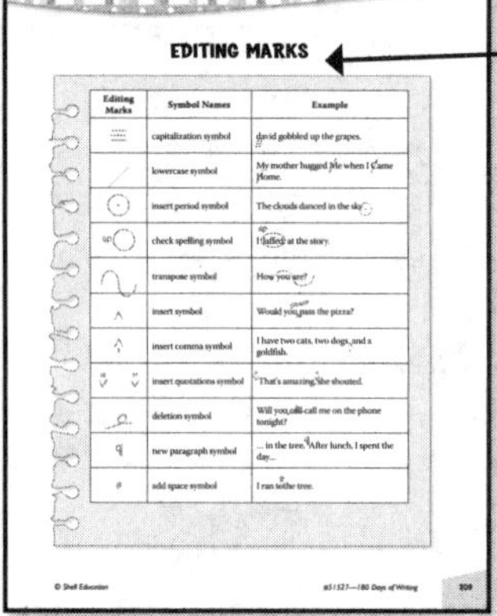

EDITING MARKS

Editing Marks	Symbol Names	Example
≡	capitalization symbol	david gobbled up the grapes.
/	lowercase symbol	My mother hugged Me when I Came Home.
⊙	insert period symbol	The clouds danced in the sky
sp○	check spelling symbol	I laffed at the story.
∽	transpose symbol	How you are?
^	insert symbol	Would you pass the pizza?
^	insert comma symbol	I have two cats, two dogs, and a goldfish.
^ ^	insert quotations symbol	That's amazing, she shouted.
	deletion symbol	Will you call call me on the phone tonight?
¶	new paragraph symbol	... in the tree. After lunch, I spent the day...
#	add space symbol	I ran tothe tree.

© Shell Education #51527—180 Days of Writing 209

Editing Marks can be found on page 209 and in the digital resources (filename: G4_editing_marks.pdf). Students may need to reference this page as they work on the editing activities (Day 4s).

If you wish to have students peer or self-edit their writing, a *Peer/Self-Editing Checklist* is provided in the digital resources (filename: G4_peer_checklist.pdf).

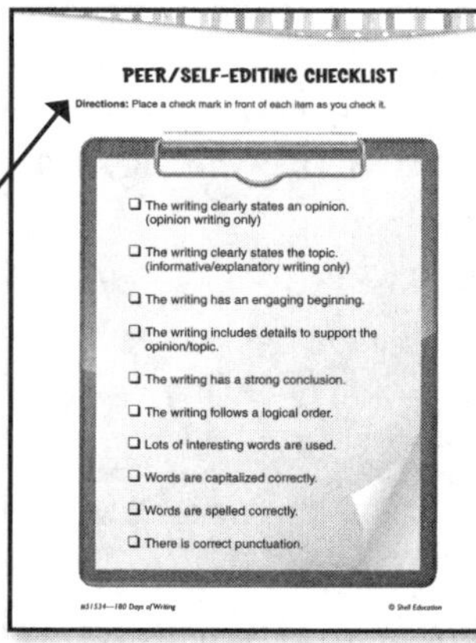

PEER/SELF-EDITING CHECKLIST

Directions: Place a check mark in front of each item as you check it.

- ❑ The writing clearly states an opinion. (opinion writing only)
- ❑ The writing clearly states the topic. (informative/explanatory writing only)
- ❑ The writing has an engaging beginning.
- ❑ The writing includes details to support the opinion/topic.
- ❑ The writing has a strong conclusion.
- ❑ The writing follows a logical order.
- ❑ Lots of interesting words are used.
- ❑ Words are capitalized correctly.
- ❑ Words are spelled correctly.
- ❑ There is correct punctuation.

Writing Signs for each of the writing genres are on pages 213–215 and in the digital resources (filename: G4_writing_signs.pdf). Hang the signs up during the appropriate two-week units to remind students which type of writing they are focusing on.

Writing Tips pages for each of the writing genres can be found on pages 210–212 and in the digital resources (filename: G4_writing_tips.pdf). Students can reference the appropriate *Writing Tips* pages as they work through the weeks.

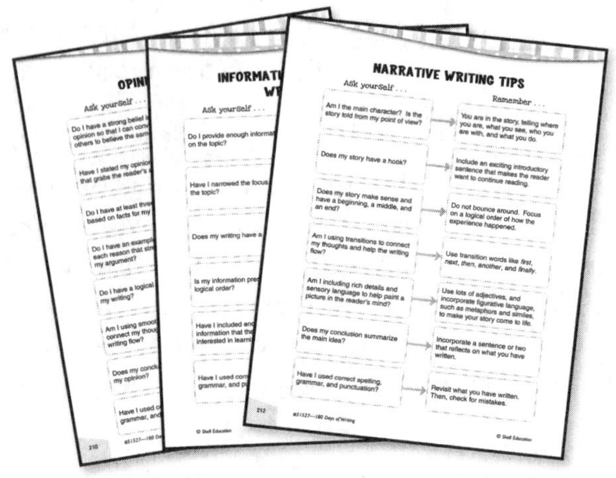

HOW TO USE THIS BOOK *(cont.)*

Diagnostic Assessment

Teachers can use the practice pages as diagnostic assessments. The data analysis tools included with the book enable teachers or parents to quickly score students' work and monitor their progress. Teachers and parents can quickly see which writing skills students may need to target further to develop proficiency.

After students complete each two-week unit, score each students' even week Day 5 published piece using the appropriate, genre-specific rubric (pages 202–204). Then, complete the *Practice Page Item Analysis* (pages 205–207) that matches the writing genre. These charts are also provided in the digital resources (filenames: G4_opinion_analysis.pdf, G4_inform_analysis.pdf, G4_narrative_analysis.pdf). Teachers can input data into the electronic files directly on the computer, or they can print the pages and analyze students' work using paper and pencil.

To Complete the Practice Page Item Analyses:

- Write or type students' names in the far-left column. Depending on the number of students, more than one copy of the form may be needed or you may need to add rows.
- The weeks in which the particular writing genres are the focus are indicated across the tops of the charts. **Note:** Students are only assessed on the even weeks, therefore the odd weeks are not included on the charts.
- For each student, record his or her rubric score in the appropriate column.
- Add the scores for each student after they've focused on a particular writing genre twice. Place that sum in the far right column. Use these scores as benchmarks to determine how each student is performing. This allows for three benchmarks during the year that you can use to gather formative diagnostic data.

HOW TO USE THIS BOOK *(cont.)*

Using the Results to Differentiate Instruction

Once results are gathered and analyzed, teachers can use the results to inform the way they differentiate instruction. The data can help determine which writing types are the most difficult for students and which students need additional instructional support and continued practice.

Whole-Class Support

The results of the diagnostic analysis may show that the entire class is struggling with a particular writing genre. If these concepts have been taught in the past, this indicates that further instruction or reteaching is necessary. If these concepts have not been taught in the past, this data is a great preassessment and may demonstrate that students do not have a working knowledge of the concepts. Thus, careful planning for the length of the unit(s) or lesson(s) must be considered, and additional front-loading may be required.

Small-Group or Individual Support

The results of the diagnostic analysis may show that an individual student or a small group of students is struggling with a particular writing genre. If these concepts have been taught in the past, this indicates that further instruction or reteaching is necessary. Consider pulling these students aside to instruct them further on the concept(s), while others are working independently. Students may also benefit from extra practice using games or computer-based resources. Teachers can also use the results to help identify individual students or groups of proficient students who are ready for enrichment or above-grade-level instruction. These students may benefit from independent learning contracts or more challenging activities.

Digital Resources

Reference page 216 for information about accessing the digital resources and an overview of the contents.

STANDARDS CORRELATIONS

Shell Education is committed to producing educational materials that are research and standards based. In this effort, we have correlated all of our products to the academic standards of all 50 states, the District of Columbia, the Department of Defense Dependents Schools, and all Canadian provinces.

How to Find Standards Correlations

To print a customized correlation report of this product for your state, visit our website at **www.tcmpub.com/shell-education** and follow the on-screen directions. If you require assistance in printing correlation reports, please contact our Customer Service Department at 1-877-777-3450.

Purpose and Intent of Standards

Legislation mandates that all states adopt academic standards that identify the skills students will learn in kindergarten through grade twelve. Many states also have standards for Pre-K. This same legislation sets requirements to ensure the standards are detailed and comprehensive.

Standards are designed to focus instruction and guide adoption of curricula. Standards are statements that describe the criteria necessary for students to meet specific academic goals. They define the knowledge, skills, and content students should acquire at each level. Standards are also used to develop standardized tests to evaluate students' academic progress.

Teachers are required to demonstrate how their lessons meet state standards. State standards are used in the development of all of our products, so educators can be assured they meet the academic requirements of each state.

The activities in this book are aligned to today's national and state-specific college and career readiness standards. The chart on page 4 lists the writing and language standards used throughout this book. A more detailed chart on pages 5–6 correlates the specific writing standards to each week.

NAME: ______________________________ **DATE:** ____________________

Directions: Read the sentences about Egyptian hieroglyphics. Place check marks next to the sentences that have specific information about hieroglyphics.

_____ Hieroglyphics use symbols and pictures.

_____ Symbols point to the beginning of a line to let the reader know where to start reading.

_____ The writing contains no punctuation.

_____ Egyptians believed cats were sacred and lucky animals.

_____ There are more than 700 symbols.

_____ Both men and women wore makeup.

_____ The Rosetta Stone helped people learn how to read the symbols.

_____ Egyptians wrote hieroglyphics on paper called *papyrus*.

NAME: ______________________ **DATE:** ______________

Directions: Read the paragraph about Egyptian hieroglyphics. Underline any sentences that are not complete.

Ancient Egyptian writing is called *hieroglyphics*. Over 700 symbols! The writing can be read in any direction, so the animal and people symbols always look toward the beginning of each line. This way, the reader knows where to start. Contains no punctuation. Hieroglyphics were a mystery until the Rosetta Stone was found in 1799. With Greek and Egyptian written side by side. Finally, people could read about the Egyptian culture!

Cursive Practice

Directions: Use cursive to write *Ancient Egypt* on the top line. Then, use cursive to write one question you have about hieroglyphics.

____

____

____

NAME: ______________________ **DATE:** ______________

Directions: Read each sentence fragment about hieroglyphics. Rewrite them as complete sentences on the lines below.

1. Beautiful to look at.

   ____

   ____

2. Early paper called *papyrus*.

   ____

   ____

3. Hard to understand.

   ____

   ____

4. Important Rosetta Stone.

   ____

   ____

Boost Your Learning!

A complete sentence needs a subject and a predicate. The **subject** is who or what the sentence is about. The **predicate** is what the subject is or does.

Example: Ancient Egypt is interesting.
(subject: Ancient Egypt) (predicate: is interesting)

NAME: ______________________ **DATE:** ______________

Directions: Use the ≡ symbol to show which words should be capitalized and the / symbol to show which words should be lowercase.

1. Egypt is in northeastern africa.
2. Makeup protected the people's Faces from the sun.
3. The nile River was important for Egyptian crops.
4. Ancient Egyptians used Toothpaste.
5. The Rosetta Stone was found by french soldiers.
6. The Egyptian Leader was called a pharaoh.

Boost Your Learning!

All **proper nouns** should be capitalized. If a letter should be capitalized, underline it three times. If a letter should be lowercase, put a line through it.

Example: The egyptians used Symbols to write.

NAME: ______________________ **DATE:** ______________

Directions: Reread the paragraph. Think about how you can improve it based on what you have practiced throughout the week. On the lines below, write three suggestions for how the author could improve the paragraph.

Ancient Egyptian writing is called *hieroglyphics*. Over 700 symbols! The writing can be read in any direction, so the animal and people symbols always look toward the beginning of each line. This way, the reader knows where to start. Contains no punctuation. Hieroglyphics were a mystery until the Rosetta Stone was found in 1799. With Greek and Egyptian written side by side. Finally, people could read about the Egyptian culture!

This week I learned: 

- to include only relevant information
- how to find and correct sentence fragments
- how to use correct capitalization

____

____

____

____

____

____

____

____

NAME: ____________________ **DATE:** ________________

Directions: Read the information about ancient Egyptian pyramids. Complete the graphic organizer with the four notes about how the pyramids were used.

- The structures were intended to protect the pharaohs' bodies forever.
- Over 130 pyramids have been found.
- Pyramids were filled with items and treasures needed for the afterlife.
- The pharaohs were buried in the pyramids.
- It took over 20 years to build each pyramid.
- Family members and servants were sometimes buried in the pyramids.

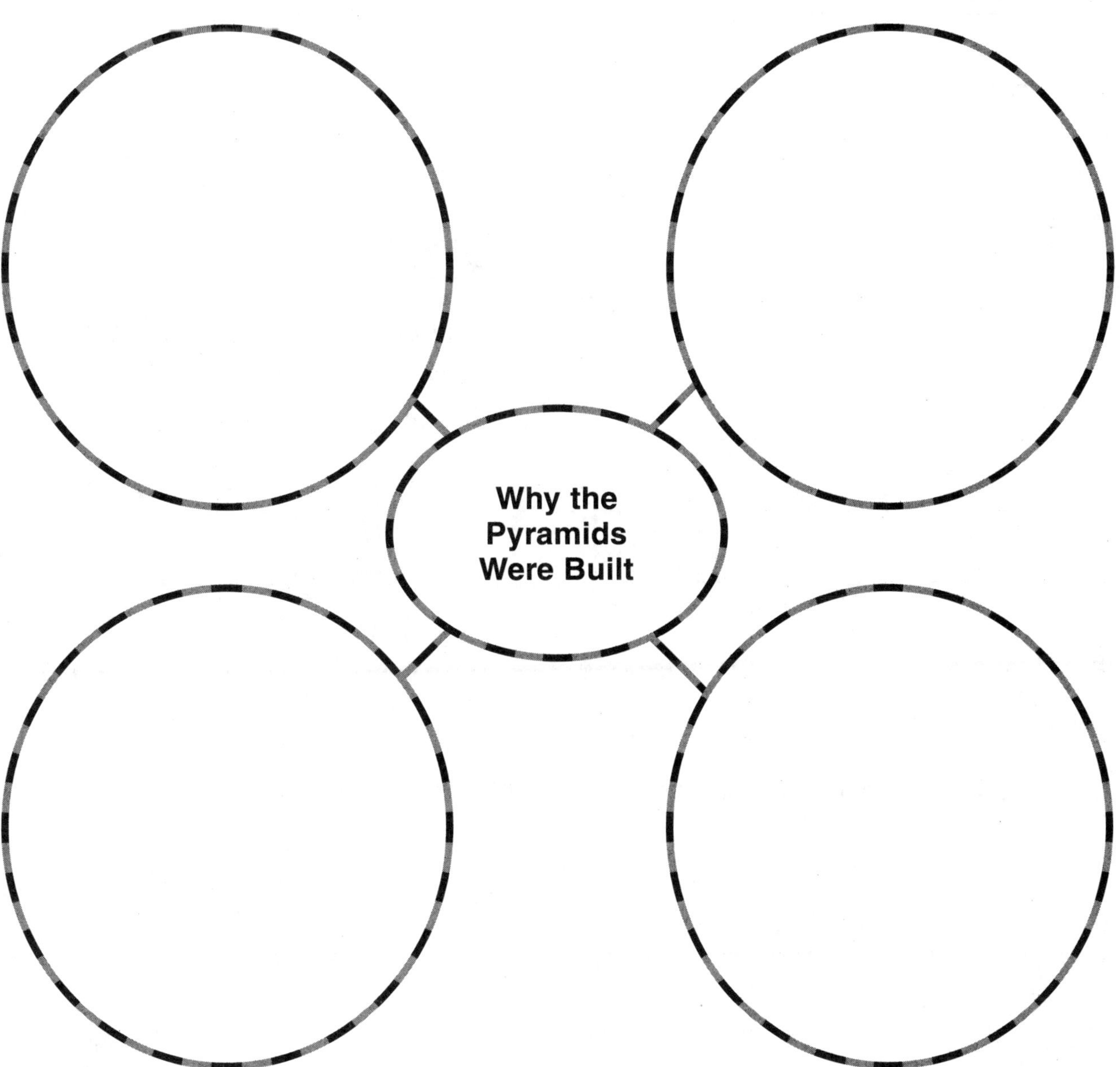

Drafting Pyramids

NAME: ______________________ **DATE:** ________________

Directions: Explain why pyramids in Egypt were built. Include what can be found in pyramids and what they are made of. Use the graphic organizer from page 19 to help you draft your informative/explanatory paragraph.

Remember!

A strong informative/explanatory paragraph should include:

- a topic sentence
- details to support the main idea
- a concluding sentence

Cursive Practice

Directions: Use cursive to write one interesting fact from your paragraph.

NAME: ______________________ **DATE:** ______________

Directions: Read each sentence. If it is a sentence fragment, put *F*. If it is a run-on, put *RO*. Rewrite the incorrect sentences.

_____ 1. The pyramids were built on the west side of the Nile River it is known as the land of the dead.

____

____

_____ 2. Built of limestone by thousands of workers.

____

____

_____ 3. The Sphinx had the head of a pharaoh it had the body of a lion.

____

____

Boost Your Learning! 

A **run-on sentence** has two sentences smashed together without proper punctuation. To fix it, you can:

- split it into two separate sentences
- use a comma and a conjunction word such as *and*, *but*, and *or*

Time to Improve! 

Look at the paragraph you wrote on page 20 about pyramids. Look for any sentence fragments or run-on sentences. If you find one, revise it!

NAME: ______________________ **DATE:** ________________

Directions: Read the paragraph. Use the ≡ or / symbols to correct the capitalization errors.

The pharaoh Tutankhamun, or "king tut," is the most famous Pharaoh of egypt. He became king at only nine years old and ruled until his death at age 18. His tomb was found in 1922 by an english Archaeologist named howard Carter. King Tut's cause of death is uncertain. Some think he died of a head injury, but most likely he died of an infection caused by a broken leg. The tomb was full of Treasures and Artifacts and taught archaeologists a lot about ancient Egypt.

Remember! 

All proper nouns should be capitalized. All regular nouns should be lowercase.

Example: egypt has a lot of History.

Time to Improve! 

Reread the paragraph you wrote on page 20 about pyramids. Look for any capitalization errors. Correct any that you find.

NAME: ______________________ **DATE:** ______________

Directions: Explain why pyramids in Egypt were built. Include what can be found in pyramids and what they are made of.

NAME: ______________________ **DATE:** ______________

Directions: Read the sentences about hurling, a popular sport in Ireland. The information needs to be organized. If the sentence is about rules, put an *R* next to it. If it is about scoring, put an *S*. If it is about players, put a *P*.

_____ 1. Players can catch and carry the ball in their hands.

_____ 2. All players are considered amateurs because there are no professional leagues.

_____ 3. Players must pass the ball by hitting it with their hurlies, or sticks, kicking it with their feet, or swatting it with their hands.

_____ 4. A team scores three points by getting the ball into the goal, which is similar to a soccer net.

_____ 5. Players do not get paid and play for pride and their love of the game.

_____ 6. One point is given if a team gets the ball over the bar at the top of the net.

NAME: ______________________ **DATE:** ______________

Directions: Read the paragraph. It has supporting facts about hurling but needs an opinion. Draft an opinion sentence to go after each fact on the lines below. The first one is done for you.

(1) Players can pass the ball using their hurley sticks, feet, or hands. (2) There are two different ways to score: into the net for three points, or over the bar at the top of the net for one point. (3) There are no professional hurling leagues, so the players do not get paid. Hurling is a fun and action-packed sport.

Opinions

1. Passing the ball in so many different ways makes hurling more interesting than other sports.

2. ____

3. ____

NAME: ______________________ **DATE:** ______________

Directions: Write the plural form of each noun.

player	______________	stick	______________
net	______________	helmet	______________
sport	______________	ball	______________
hurley	______________	team	______________
bail	______________	hand	______________

Directions: Write two sentences using at least three plural nouns from above.

1. ____

____

____

2. ____

____

____

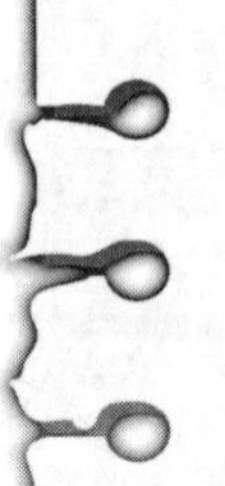

Boost Your Learning!

To make most **nouns plural**, add *-s* to the ends of the words. If a noun ends with a *-y*, change the *-y* to *-i* and add *-es*.

Examples
point ➔ points
buddy ➔ buddies

NAME: ____________________ **DATE:** ________________

Directions: Read the sentences. Each one contains a helping verb and a main verb. Circle the helping verbs and underline the main verbs.

1. Players may hit the ball with hurley sticks.
2. Hurlers must run fast to play this sport.
3. Teams may earn up to three points with one score.
4. A player must have fast reflexes in hurling.
5. The amateur players may receive money.

Boost Your Learning!

A **main verb** tells the main action in a sentence.
Examples: *speak*, *jump*, *run*

A **helping verb** helps extend the meaning of the main verb.
Examples: *should*, *could*, *must*, *will*, *may*, *might*

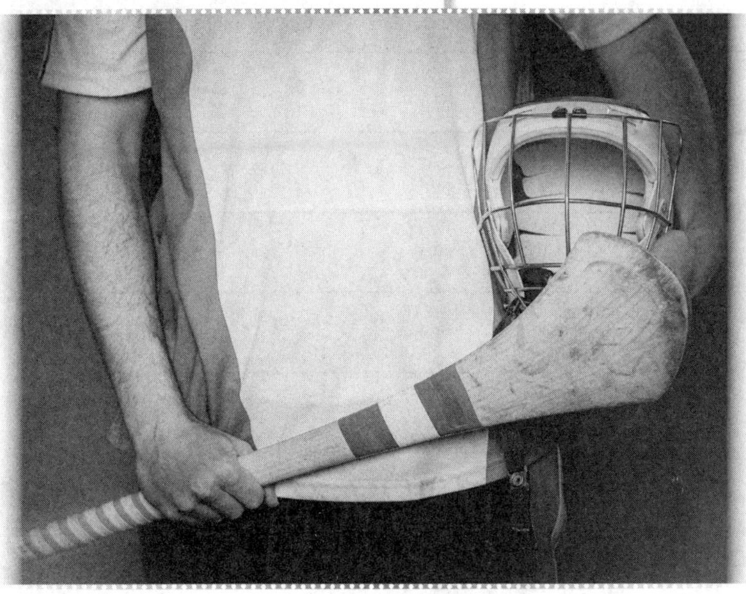

NAME: ______________________ **DATE:** ______________

Publishing

Hurling

Directions: Revisit the paragraph. Use what you have learned throughout the week to write a final version of it.

Players can pass the ball using their hurley sticks, feet, or hands. There are two different ways to score: into the net for three points, or over the bar at the top of the net for one point. There are no professional hurling leagues, so the players do not get paid. Hurling is a fun and action-packed sport.

This week I learned:

- to organize my ideas
- how to add opinions
- how to use helping verbs
- how to spell plural nouns

NAME: ______________________ **DATE:** ______________

Directions: Cricket is a game similar to baseball. Read the chart that compares the two sports. Then, complete the questions below.

Cricket	Baseball
• 11 players • games last six hours to five days • batsmen wear helmets and pads on the legs and chest • bats are long, wide, and flat • popular in England, India, Pakistan, Australia, and New Zealand	• 9 players • games last about three hours • batters wear helmets, gloves, and optional shin pads • bats are long, round like a baton, and tapered at the end • popular in the United States, Canada, the Caribbean, Japan, and the Philippines

1. Which sport would you rather play?

____

2. Give three ideas to support your opinion.

- ____
  ____
- ____
  ____
- ____
  ____

NAME: ______________________ **DATE:** ______________

Directions: There are many aspects to the sport of cricket. Explain your opinions on the rules and the players involved in the sport. Use your notes from page 29 to help you draft your opinion paragraph.

Remember!

To write a strong opinion paragraph, remember to include:

- an introductory sentence stating your opinion
- support for your opinion
- a concluding sentence

Cursive Practice

Directions: Use cursive to write a sentence about something you enjoy doing.

NAME: ______________________ **DATE:** ______________

Directions: Rewrite each sentence correctly using the plural form of each underlined noun. **Note:** Two verbs will have to change to match the plural nouns.

1. Joseph will write his essay about the <u>rule</u> of cricket.

____

____

2. The <u>lady</u> brings the <u>baby</u> to watch cricket.

____

____

3. The <u>victory</u> belongs to the <u>player</u>.

____

____

Remember! 

To make most nouns plural, add *-s*. If a noun ends in a *-y*, change the *-y* to *-i* and add *-es*.

Time to Improve! 

Reread the opinion paragraph you wrote on page 30. Look for any misspelled words, especially plural nouns. Correct any mistakes you find.

NAME: ______________________ **DATE:** ________________

Directions: Read the paragraph. Circle any helping verbs you find.

Every four years, cricket teams from around the world compete in the Cricket World Cup. Players must battle on the field in the hope that they might be crowned world champions. England hosted the first three tournaments in 1975, 1979, and 1983. Officials knew everyone should have the opportunity to host the World Cup, so India and Pakistan hosted in 1987. The modern Cricket World Cup trophy was designed in 1999. Before that, each trophy would have been a unique design. Now, each Cup trophy is identical except that the winning team's name is engraved on it.

Remember! 

A helping verb helps extend the meaning of the main verb. **Examples:** *can, could, may, might, will, would, must, shall, should,* and *ought to*

Time to Improve! 

Reread the opinion paragraph you wrote on page 30. Are any helping verbs included? If so, make sure they are used properly and make sense.

NAME: ______________________ DATE: ________________

Directions: There are many aspects to the sport cricket. Explain your opinions on the rules and the players involved in the sport.

NAME: ______________________ **DATE:** ______________

Directions: Read the sensory details about cupcakes. Then, copy each detail into the correct column on the table. Add some of your own sensory details, too!

Sensory Details

pink frosting	vanilla	lit candle	sugar
crinkly wrapper	sprinkles	chocolate	moist
sticky frosting	warm	large	sweet

See	Taste/Smell	Feel

NAME: ____________________________ **DATE:** ___________________

Directions: Read the narrative paragraph about a cupcake. Underline the sensory details.

As everyone finished singing, Jada looked at the cupcake sitting in front of her. A lit, glowing candle sat in the middle of the sprinkles scattered on the icing. After making her wish and blowing out the candle, Jada peeled back the crinkly wrapper. A bit of frosting stuck to her lip as she bit into the chocolate cake. It was sweet and delicious. She noticed her friends were all enjoying their cupcakes, as well. Breathing in the scent of vanilla, she took another bite. Jada enjoyed every bite of her birthday cupcake.

Cursive Practice *abc*

Directions: Use cursive to write the word *cupcakes*. Then, use cursive to write three ingredients you might need to bake some cupcakes.

______________________________ ______________________________

______________________________ ______________________________

NAME: ______________________ **DATE:** ______________

Directions: Rewrite each boring sentence by adding adjectives and sensory details.

Boring: I smell the baking cookies. **New and Improved:**	**Boring:** I hear the oven timer. **New and Improved:**
Boring: I touch the cookie sheet. **New and Improved:**	**Boring:** I see the sprinkles. **New and Improved:**

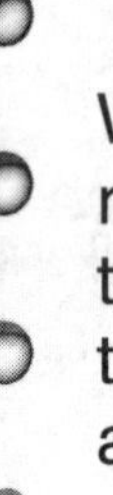

Boost Your Learning!

When focusing on **sensory details**, you want the reader to imagine what the topic looks, smells, tastes, sounds, and feels like. **Adjectives**, words that describe or modify something or someone, are a great way to make your writing come to life!

Example: *I taste the cookie* can be changed to *I taste the delicious and gooey cookie*.

NAME: ____________________ **DATE:** ____________

Directions: Read each sentence. If it is declarative, write *D* on the line. If it is imperative, write *IM*. If it is interrogative, write *IN*. If it is exclamatory, write *E*. Then, add the correct punctuation mark to the end of each sentence.

_____ 1. The cupcakes are burning__

_____ 2. Can you open the oven door__

_____ 3. I can't believe we ran out of eggs__

_____ 4. The spatula is in the drawer__

_____ 5. Wipe up the spilled milk__

_____ 6. How much longer should it bake__

_____ 7. Put the butter in the refrigerator__

_____ 8. The cookies should cool for 10 minutes__

Boost Your Learning!

Different types of sentences include:

Declarative—a telling sentence **Example:** The oven needs to be preheated to 350 degrees.	**Imperative**—a commanding sentence **Example:** Add sugar to the batter.
Interrogative—an asking sentence **Example:** Would you like chocolate or vanilla?	**Exclamatory**—an exciting sentence **Example:** This dessert is delicious!

NAME: ______________________________ **DATE:** ____________________

Directions: Read the paragraph. Then, answer the question.

As everyone finished singing, Jada looked at the cupcake sitting in front of her. A lit candle sat in the middle of the sprinkles scattered on the icing. After making her wish and blowing out the candle, Jada peeled back the crinkly wrapper. She wondered what was inside her biggest gift. A bit of frosting stuck to her lip as she bit into the chocolate cake. It was sweet and delicious. She noticed her friends were all enjoying their cupcakes, as well. Breathing in the scent of vanilla, she took another bite. Her mother began serving juice to the guests. Jada enjoyed every bite of her birthday cupcake.

This week I learned: 

- to include information about the topic
- how to use sensory details and adjectives
- how to identify different types of sentences

1. Does the author stay on topic? How do you know?

____

____

____

____

NAME: ______________________ **DATE:** ________________

Directions: Imagine eating an ice cream cone. Brainstorm sensory details to describe the experience. Complete the graphic organizer with at least two details in each box.

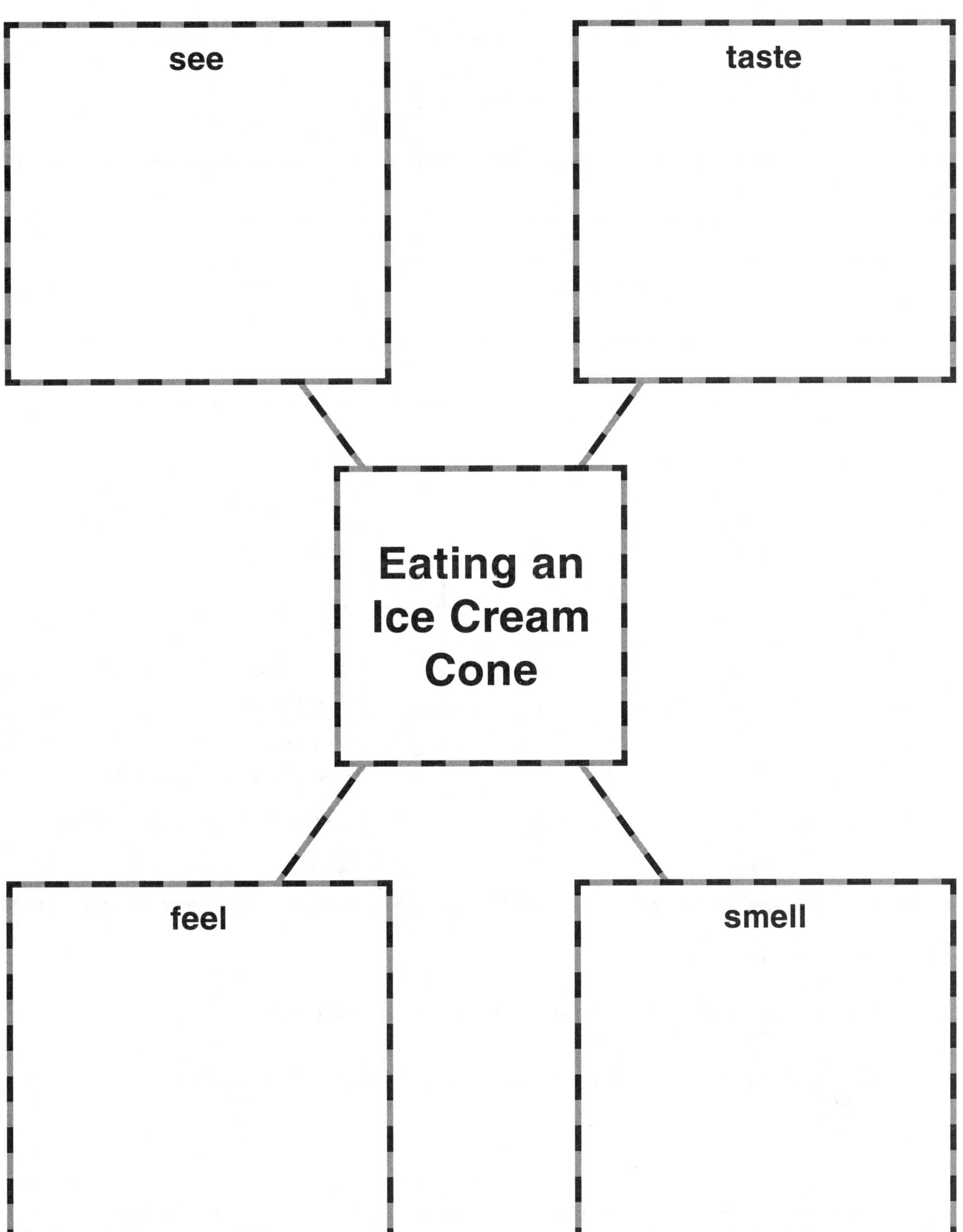

NAME: ______________________ **DATE:** ________________

Drafting: Ice Cream

Directions: Describe a time you were eating an ice cream cone. Include what the ice cream looked like and how it felt, tasted, and smelled. Use your notes on page 39 to help you draft your narrative paragraph.

Remember! 

A strong narrative paragraph:

- includes an introductory and a concluding sentence
- uses sensory details to describe the experience
- makes it sound like a story

Cursive Practice

Directions: Use cursive to complete the following sentence:

My favorite ice cream flavor is...

NAME: ____________________ **DATE:** ______________

Directions: Read each jumbled sentence. Rewrite each one correctly on the lines. The first word in each sentence is capitalized for you. Then, underline any adjectives in the sentences.

1. warm and taste Crisp delicious cones

____

____

2. days Frozen melts ice cream on hot

____

____

3. fun are fruity Strawberries choices

____

____

4. ingredients tasty flavors fresh Natural make and

____

____

Time to Improve! 

Reread the narrative you wrote on page 40. See if there are any places you can add adjectives to bring your sensory details to life! If you have more than one adjective describing something, make sure the words are in an order that makes sense.

NAME: ______________________ **DATE:** ______________

Directions: Read the paragraph. Find four sentences that have the wrong ending punctuation. Use the ℘ symbol to delete the incorrect punctuation and the ∧ symbol to insert the correct punctuation.

People eat ice cream cones every day! But when was the cone invented. Although several different stories tell of its beginning, most Americans believe the legend of the 1904 World's Fair in St. Louis. A street vendor curled a warm wafer cookie into a cone shape and served ice cream in it. This allowed people to eat their ice cream on the go. Though this may not have really been the first time a cone was used, it became very popular after this event. Now, cones are everywhere. The next time you have an ice cream cone, remember the 1904 World's Fair?

Time to Improve! 

Reread the narrative paragraph you wrote on page 40 about eating ice cream. Check that your sentences end with the correct punctuation marks. If there are any errors, correct them.

NAME: ______________________ **DATE:** ________________

Directions: Describe a time you were eating an ice cream cone. Include what the ice cream looked like and how it felt, tasted, and smelled.

NAME: ______________________ **DATE:** ______________

Directions: Read the information in the web about the human skeleton. Place check marks in the bubbles that relate to the topic.

Human Skeleton

- Babies have 300 bones, but adults have 206.
- The nose and ears are made of cartilage.
- The longest bone in the body is the thighbone, which is called the femur.
- Bones in the hands and feet make up over half of the body's bones.
- Many insects have exoskeletons.
- Humans have many parts to their bodies.
- Teeth are not considered part of the skeleton.
- The smallest bone in the body is in the ear. It is smaller than a grain of rice.
- Birds have hollow bones.

NAME: ______________________ **DATE:** ______________

Directions: This informative/explanatory paragraph about the human skeleton is missing something! Read the paragraph. Then, draft your own introductory sentence and concluding sentence.

Introductory Sentence

____

____

When babies are born, thcy have around 300 bones. As they grow, some bones fuse together. By adulthood, people have 206 bones. The longest bone is the thighbone, which is called the femur. The stapes bone in the ear is the smallest bone. The hands and feet have many bones. More than half of the body's bones are in these two locations alone!

Concluding Sentence

____

____

Cursive Practice *abc*

Directions: Write the following four bones in cursive: *stapes*, *rib*, *skull*, and *pelvis*.

____________________ ____________________

____________________ ____________________

NAME: ______________________________ **DATE:** ____________________

Directions: Read the paragraph about the human skeleton. Choose the correct linking phrases from the Linking Phrase Bank, and insert them into the paragraph above the ^ symbols.

Linking Phrase Bank

On the other hand, | For example, | In fact,

The human skeleton is fascinating. ^ when babies are born, they have around 300 bones. As they grow, some bones fuse together. By adulthood, people have 206 bones. The longest bone is the thighbone, which is called the femur. ^ the stapes bone in the ear is the smallest bone. The hands and feet have many bones. ^ more than half of the body's bones are in those two locations alone! The skeleton provides support to the whole body.

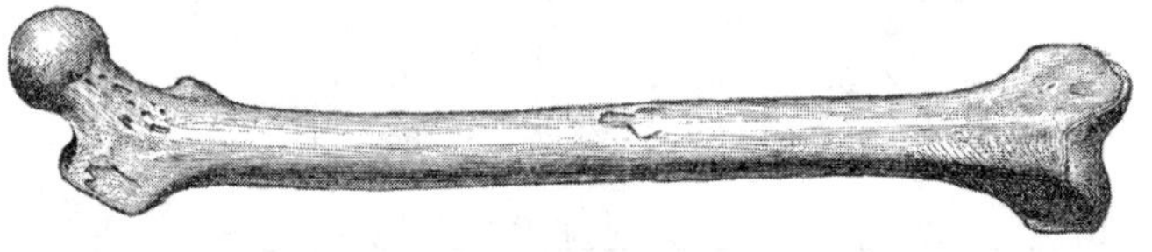

Boost Your Learning!

Linking words help guide readers through your writing. They make connections and link ideas together.

because
Example: Ribs are important ^ they protect organs.

NAME: ______________________________ **DATE:** ____________________

Directions: Read the dictionary definitions for the word *fuse*. Then, answer the questions.

fuse \fyooz\

1. *noun.* a device that causes electricity to stop flowing if the current reaches an unsafe level
2. *noun.* a string connected to an explosive device (like a firecracker) that is lit on fire
3. *verb.* to join different things together

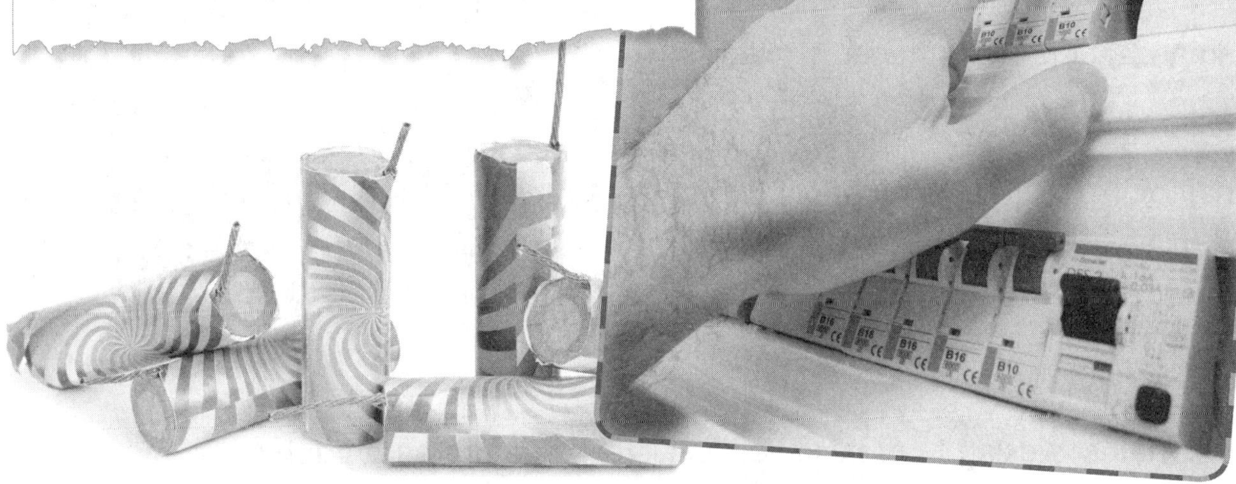

1. Read this sentence: *When babies are born, they have around 300 bones, but as they grow, some bones <u>fuse</u> together.* Which definition of the word *fuse* is being used in this sentence? _____
2. Read this sentence: *My dad had to go find the <u>fuse</u> box when the electricity went out during the storm.* Which definition of the word *fuse* is being used in this sentence? _____
3. Write a sentence for the definition of *fuse* that has not been used yet.

____

____

NAME: ______________________ **DATE:** ______________

Directions: Read the paragraph. Then, answer the questions.

When babies are born, they have around 300 bones, but as they grow, some bones fuse together. By adulthood, people have 206 bones. The longest bone is the thighbone, which is called the femur. On the other hand, the stapes bone in the ear is the smallest bone. The hands and feet have many bones. In fact, more than half of the body's bones are in these two locations alone!

This week I learned: 

- to write introductory and concluding sentences
- to use linking words

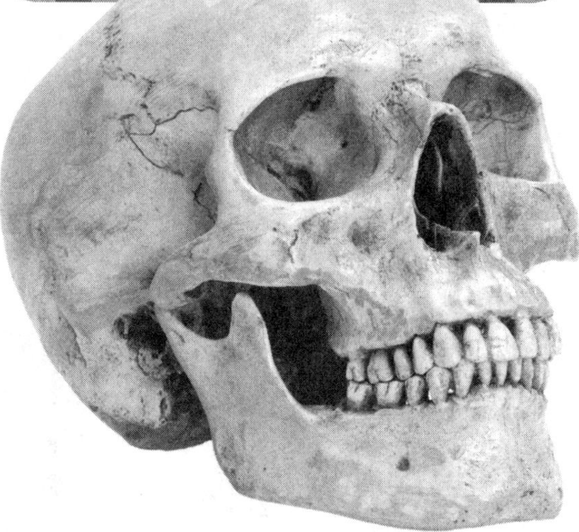

1. What is missing from this informative/explanatory paragraph?

____

____

____

2. Does this paragraph inform you about a topic? How?

____

____

____

NAME: ______________________ **DATE:** ________________

Directions: Read the information about the three different types of muscles. Place check marks in the bubbles that relate only to the three types of muscles.

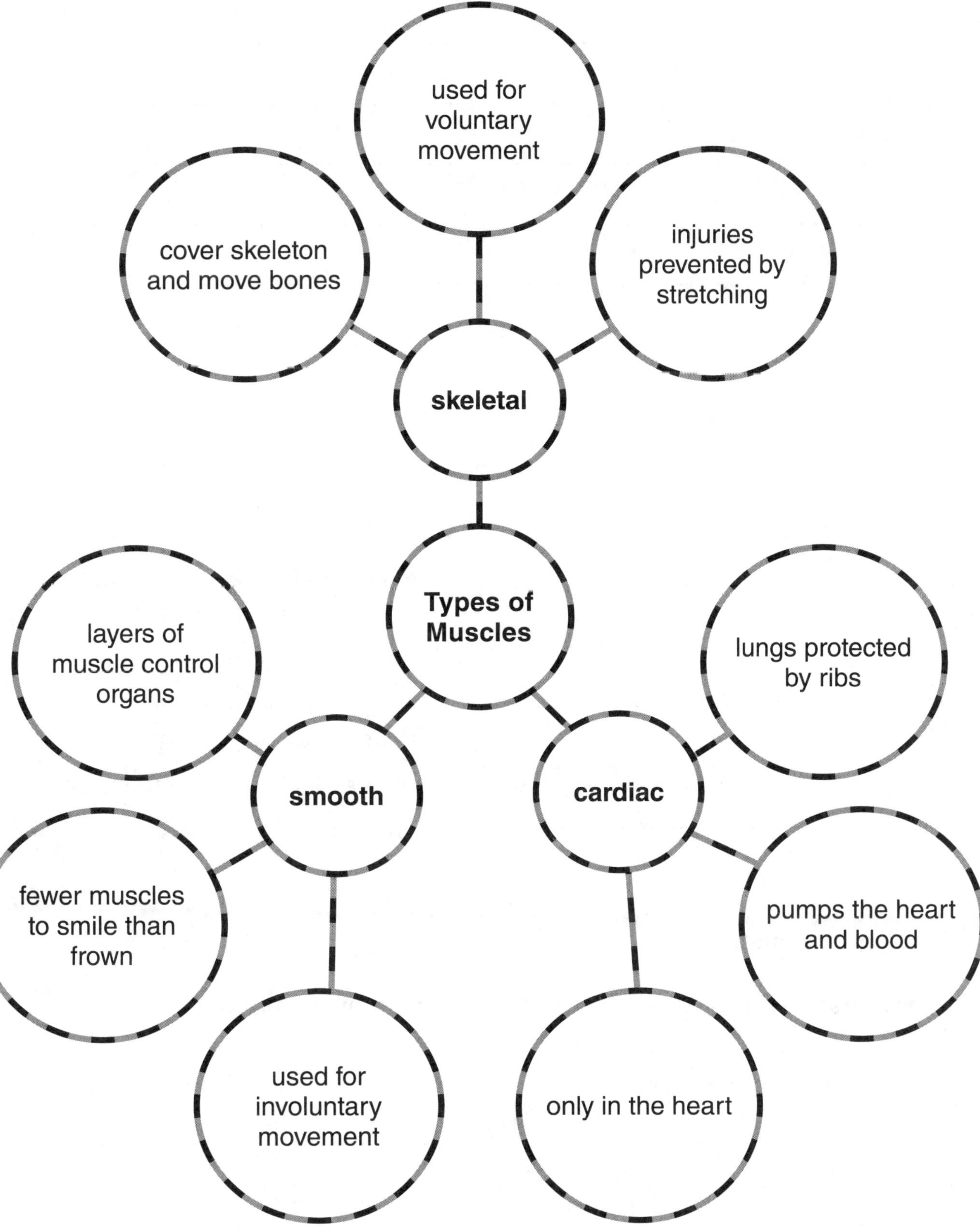

NAME: ____________________ **DATE:** ____________

Directions: Explain what human muscles are. Include some types of muscles and their functions. Use the web from page 49 to help you draft your informative/explanatory paragraph.

Remember!

A strong informative/explanatory paragraph should include:

- only relevant information
- an introductory and a concluding sentence
- details to support the topic

Cursive Practice *abc*

Directions: Use cursive to write one fact you know about muscles.

NAME: ______________________ **DATE:** ________________

Directions: Read the sentences. Shade in the circle for the linking word or phrase that sounds best in each sentence. Then, write it on the line.

Word Bank		
since	in addition to	but
for example	On the other hand	

1. Exercising different muscles is important. ______________________, a person could do sit ups one day and push ups the next.

2. ______________________ the heart beats all of the time, the cardiac muscle never gets a rest.

3. Kicking uses voluntary muscles. ______________________, digesting food uses involuntary muscles.

4. It takes only 17 muscles to smile ______________________ 43 muscles to frown.

5. ______________________ making your muscles stronger, exercise can also warm you up on a cold day.

Time to Improve! 

Reread the paragraph you wrote on page 50. Does it have any linking words or phrases? If not, see if you can add some to help guide the reader through your writing. Use the ^ symbol to insert linking words or phrases.

NAME: ______________________ **DATE:** ______________

Directions: Read the definitions for the word *body*. Then, write a sentence for each definition.

body \bah-dee\

1. *noun.* the bones, flesh, and organs of a person or animal
2. *noun.* a large area of water
3. *noun.* the main part of something written

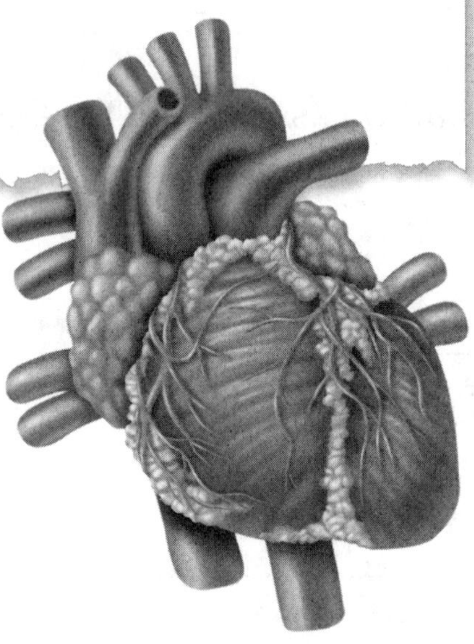

Definition 1: ____

____

____

Definition 2: ____

____

____

Definition 3: ____

____

____

NAME: ______________________ **DATE:** ________________

Directions: Explain what human muscles are. Include some types of muscles and their functions.

NAME: ______________________ **DATE:** ________________

Directions: Read the information about Morse code. If the information is an advantage of using Morse code, write an *A* on the line. If it is a disadvantage, write a *D*.

_____ 1. secure communication because not everyone knows Morse code

_____ 2. understood universally in all countries

_____ 3. slow compared to modern technology

_____ 4. Equipment is inexpensive.

_____ 5. Transmitting messages is easy.

_____ 6. Training is needed to send and receive messages.

_____ 7. time consuming to spell each word

NAME: ______________________ **DATE:** ______________

Directions: Read the opinion paragraph about keeping Morse code in modern times. Underline details that support the author's opinion.

Though considered outdated by some people, Morse code should still be used in modern times. Morse code was invented by Samuel Morse in the 1830s. He sent the first message from Washington, D.C., to Baltimore. Communicating through this code is fairly secure. Because not everyone knows it, it is unlikely the message will fall into the wrong hands. The equipment is inexpensive and transmitting messages is easy. It is slow and time-consuming, though. Morse code is used all over the world and is understood by receivers in all countries, no matter what language they speak. There are many great things about modern technology, but Morse code still has a place in today's communication.

Cursive Practice

Directions: Use cursive to write *Morse code* on the top line. Then, use cursive to write the words *send* and *receive* on the bottom lines.

____

______________________ ______________________

NAME: ______________________ **DATE:** ________________

Directions: Read the sentences. The underlined words could use context clues to better understand them. Rewrite the sentences to include context clues.

1. Though considered outdated by some people, Morse code should still be used in modern times.

____

____

____

____

2. The equipment is inexpensive and transmitting messages is easy.

____

____

____

____

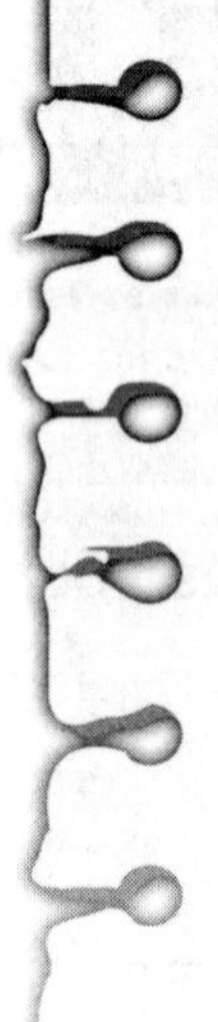

Boost Your Learning!

Context clues help you figure out tricky words or phrases as you read. They often involve one of the following:

- **a definition**—*The receiver sits at a telegraph, which is device that sends messages.*
- **an example**—*Sending the coded messages can be tedious, like counting grains of rice.*
- **a restatement**—*Many messages during battle are encoded or put into code to keep them secret.*

NAME: ______________________ **DATE:** ______________

Directions: Read the sentences. The underlined words are used incorrectly. Use the ℘ symbol to correct them. Then, write your own sentence below.

1. The station could not <u>except</u> the telegram because of bad weather.

2. Do not <u>loose</u> the message before we can translate it from Morse code!

3. <u>Their</u> going to take a class to learn Morse code.

4. The <u>capitol</u> city receives important telegrams.

5. Be sure to translate the <u>hole</u> telegram.

6. Write your own sentence using the homophone pair *two* and *too*.

____

____

Boost Your Learning!

Homophones are words that sound the same but have different meanings. They may or may not be spelled the same.

Example: *knew* and *new*

NAME: ______________________ **DATE:** ______________

Directions: Reread the opinion paragraph. Think about what you have learned this week. On the lines below, write at least three ways you can improve this writing.

Though considered outdated by some people, Morse code should still be used in modern times. Morse code was invented by Samuel Morse in the 1830s. He sent the first message from Washington, D.C., to Baltimore. Communicating through this code is fairly secure. Because not everyone knows it, it is unlikely the message will fall into the wrong hands. Also, the equipment needed is inexpensive and transmitting messages is easy. It is slow and time-consuming, though. Morse code is used all over the world and is understood by receivers in all countries, no matter what language they speak. There are many great things about modern technology, but Morse code still has a place in today's communication.

____

____

____

____

____

____

____

____

____

____

This week I learned:

- to include only relevant information
- to use context clues when writing

NAME: ____________________ DATE: ______________

Directions: Read the information about telegrams and emails. Then, brainstorm some thoughts and opinions you have about each one.

A **telegram** is a form of communication sent by a telegraph. An operator receives the message, writes it down, and then it is hand-delivered to the recipient. The messages are usually very short and contain emergency information.

- ______________________________
- ______________________________
- ______________________________
- ______________________________

An **email** is a form of communication sent over the Internet using an electronic device. The sender types a message, sends it to an email address, and the email appears on the recipient's electronic device. Messages vary in length and can be about any subject.

- ______________________________
- ______________________________
- ______________________________
- ______________________________

NAME: ______________________ **DATE:** ________________

Directions: Would you rather receive a telegram or an email? Explain why you would want to receive one over the other. Use the notes from page 59 to help you draft your opinion paragraph.

Remember!

A strong opinion paragraph should:

- begin with an introductory sentence that states your opinion
- include details that support your opinion
- end with a concluding sentence

Cursive Practice

Directions: Use cursive to write the word *telegram*. Then, use cursive to write the names of three people who you think would enjoy receiving telegrams.

NAME: ______________________ **DATE:** ________________

Directions: Read the sentences with context clues that help explain the underlined words. Then, answer the questions.

1. The noise from the room agitated Myra because she was trying to concentrate on her message.

   What does *agitated* mean? How did the context clue help you figure it out?

   ____

   ____

   ____

2. The superfluous message was two pages long but could have been one.

   What does *superfluous* mean? How did the context clue help you figure it out?

   ____

   ____

   ____

3. The operator was very attentive, or paid close attention, when receiving the telegram message.

   What does *attentive* mean? How did the context clue help you figure it out?

   ____

   ____

   ____

Time to Improve! 

Read the paragraph you wrote on page 60. Look for words your reader might not know. Consider adding context clues to help clarify those tricky words!

NAME: ______________________ **DATE:** ________________

Directions: Read each pair of homophones. Write one sentence that includes both words for each pair.

1. *heir* and *air*

____

____

2. *knows* and *nose*

____

____

3. *hole* and *whole*

____

____

4. *piece* and *peace*

____

____

5. *right* and *write*

____

____

Time to Improve! 

Reread the opinion paragraph you wrote on page 60. Do you have any homophones? If so, make sure you have used them correctly.

NAME: ______________________ **DATE:** ________________

Directions: Would you rather receive a telegram or an email? Explain why you would want to receive one over the other.

NAME: ______________________ **DATE:** ______________

Directions: Read the facts about Great Danes, a breed of dog. All of the information is true, but there are too many facts for one paragraph. Place check marks next to three to five facts you think are important to include in an informative/explanatory paragraph about a Great Dane's physical characteristics.

Facts

_____ one of the largest dog breeds

_____ known as "gentle giant" and "Apollo of dogs"

_____ good with children

_____ life expectancy is about eight years

_____ originally a hunting dog, now a pet

_____ males are 120 to 200 pounds (54 to 91 kilograms), females are 100 to 130 pounds (45 to 59 kilograms)

_____ 2014 *Guinness Book of World Records'* largest dog

_____ colors are: black, fawn (yellow gold with black "mask" on face), brindle (fawn and black swirled together), and harlequin (white with large black marks)

_____ needs a daily walk but not a high exercise breed

_____ ears can be cropped (cut so they stand up to a point) or natural (floppy)

_____ average litter is six to eight puppies

NAME: ______________________________ **DATE:** ____________________

Directions: Read the paragraph about the physical characteristics of Great Danes. Then, answer the question below.

The Great Dane is a dog breed known as "the gentle giant." They are gentle with children and make good family pets. They are one of the largest breeds of dog in the world. The 2014 world record for largest dog was a Great Dane named Zeus. Originally, they were used for hunting, but now they are mainly pets. Males are between 120 to 200 pounds (54 to 91 kilograms), females are 100 to 130 pounds (45 to 59 kilograms). Their ears are naturally floppy, but they are sometimes cropped so they stand up to a point. The life expectancy for a Great Dane is about eight years. They can have four different types of coats: black, fawn (yellow gold with black "mask" on face), brindle (fawn and black swirled together), and harlequin (white with large black marks). Great Danes make wonderful—and big—pets!

1. Underline one sentence you think should not be in the draft. Why does it not belong?

____

____

____

Cursive Practice *abc*

Directions: Use cursive to write one fact about Great Danes.

____

____

NAME: ______________________ **DATE:** ________________

Directions: Read each sentence. If it is correct, put a *C* on the line. If it is a run-on, put *RO* on the line. Correct any run-ons with commas and conjunctions.

_____ 1. Great Danes have short hair it requires brushing once a week.

____

____

_____ 2. Cropping a Great Dane's ears is illegal in most of Europe.

____

____

_____ 3. Great Danes need daily walks they are not high exercise dogs.

____

____

_____ 4. This breed needs to be around people it could get anxious.

____

____

Remember! 

A run-on sentence happens when two full sentences are put together without punctuation. To correct one, insert a comma and a conjunction like *and*, *but*, and *or*.

Example: Pets teach responsibility**,** *and* they bring joy to families.

NAME: ______________________________ **DATE:** ____________________

Directions: Read the sentences. Complete each sentence with the progressive verb *will be* or *were*. Use context clues to help you know which verb to use.

1. Tomorrow the family ________________ taking the dog to the vet.

2. The puppies ________________ whining when they saw their food.

3. The kids ________________ playing with the dog until lunch is ready.

4. Yesterday, the dogs ________________ eating out of each other's bowls.

Boost Your Learning!

The **progressive verb tense** shows continuing action. To form this tense, use the helping "to be" verb and the *-ing* verb.

Examples

Lisa **was chasing** her dog all over the neighborhood.

She **is teaching** her dog the "come" command.

After he learns it, he **will be running** to her every time she calls him.

NAME: ______________________ **DATE:** ________________

Directions: Think about what you have learned this week. Write notes in the margins about what makes this paragraph strong.

The Great Dane is a dog breed known as "the gentle giant." They are gentle with children and make good family pets. They are one of the largest breeds of dog in the world. Originally, they were used for hunting, but now they are mainly pets. Males are between 120 to 200 pounds (54 to 91 kilograms), and females are 100 to 130 pounds (45 to 59 kilograms). Their ears are naturally floppy, but they are sometimes cropped so they stand up to a point. The life expectancy for a Great Dane is about eight years. They can have four different types of coats: black, fawn (yellow gold with black "mask" on face), brindle (fawn and black swirled together), and harlequin (white with large black marks). Great Danes make wonderful—and big—pets!

This week I learned: 

- to include strong details that support the main idea
- to correct run-on sentences with commas and conjunctions
- to use correct verb tenses

NAME: ______________________ **DATE:** ______________

Directions: Read the main topics for an informative/explanatory paragraph on the Chihuahua, a breed of dog. Choose one topic and put a check mark by it. Then, read the facts. Put stars by the facts that support the topic you chose.

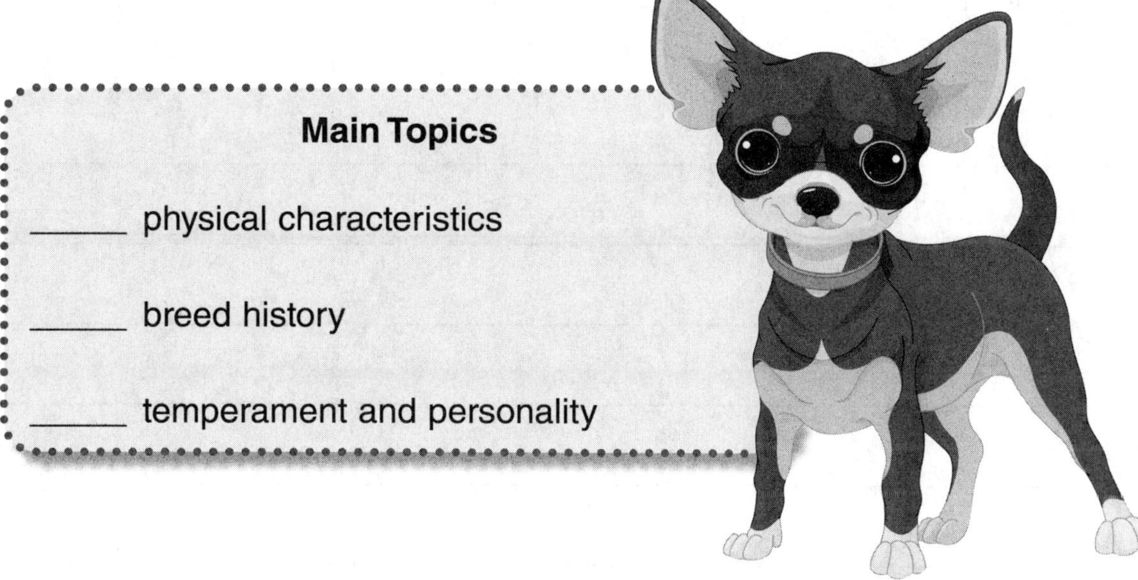

Main Topics

_____ physical characteristics

_____ breed history

_____ temperament and personality

Facts

_____ smallest breed of dog weighing 4 to 6 pounds (2 to 3 kilograms)

_____ clay pots with dogs resembling modern Chihuahuas were found in Mexico from 100 C.E.

_____ can be long- or short-haired

_____ considered a difficult breed to housebreak, or train

_____ named after a state in Mexico called Chihuahua

_____ intelligent and loyal to its owner

_____ life expectancy of 12 to 20 years

_____ possibly descended from the Fennec fox, which is small with big eyes and ears

_____ coats can be any color, either solid or multicolored

_____ like to burrow in pillows and blankets

Drafting
Chihuahuas

NAME: ______________________ **DATE:** ______________

Directions: Write a paragraph about Chihuahuas. Include specific facts about the breed, including their physical characteristics, breed history, and personality. Use the notes from page 69 to help you draft your informative/explanatory paragraph.

____

____

____

____

____

____

____

____

____

____

____

____

____

Remember!

A strong informative/explanatory paragraph should include:

- an introductory and a concluding sentence
- details that support the main idea

Cursive Practice

Directions: Write the following words in cursive: *Chihuahua*, *Mexico*, and *Fennec fox*.

____

____

____

NAME: ______________________ **DATE:** ________________

Directions: Read the paragraph. Look for run-on sentences. Use the ∧ symbol to insert commas and conjunction words.

Newborn puppies are cute they need a lot of help during their first few weeks. The pups are born blind, deaf, and toothless. They cannot even maintain their body temperature they huddle together to stay warm. In the first week, they double their body weight and spend 90 percent of their time sleeping. After about two weeks, the puppies' sealed ears and eyes open at three weeks, they begin to walk. Before long, the pups are running and playing together.

Time to Improve! 

Reread the paragraph you wrote on page 70 about Chihuahuas. Do you have any run-on sentences? If so, make sure you correct them.

NAME: ____________________ **DATE:** ________________

Directions: Write the correct progressive verb tense for each sentence. Each answer should have a helping verb and the *-ing* form of the given verb. The first one has been done for you.

Past Tense

1. The puppies were eating all of the food. (eat)

2. The owner ________________ (think) it was time to feed them more food.

Present Tense

3. Today, he ________________ (feed) them twice as much food.

4. The puppies ________________ (gobble) up every last bit.

Future Tense

5. Tomorrow, the owner ________________ (shop) for extra bags of dog food.

6. The puppies ________________ (grow) faster than ever!

Time to Improve! 

Look at the paragraph you wrote on page 70. Pay careful attention to the verb tenses. Do you have any progressive verbs in your writing? If so, make sure they are used correctly.

NAME: ______________________________ **DATE:** ____________________

Directions: Write a paragraph about Chihuahuas. Include specific facts about the breed, including their physical characteristics, breed history, and personality.

NAME: ______________________ **DATE:** ________________

Directions: Below are ideas for a narrative paragraph about hiking in Yosemite National Park in California. Decide if the notes belong in the beginning, middle, or end of the paragraph. Then, copy them into the correct sections.

- stop at a stream for water
- gather hiking supplies at camp
- see deer, fox, and bobcat while hiking
- walk back to camp
- climb to the top of the mountain and look out over land

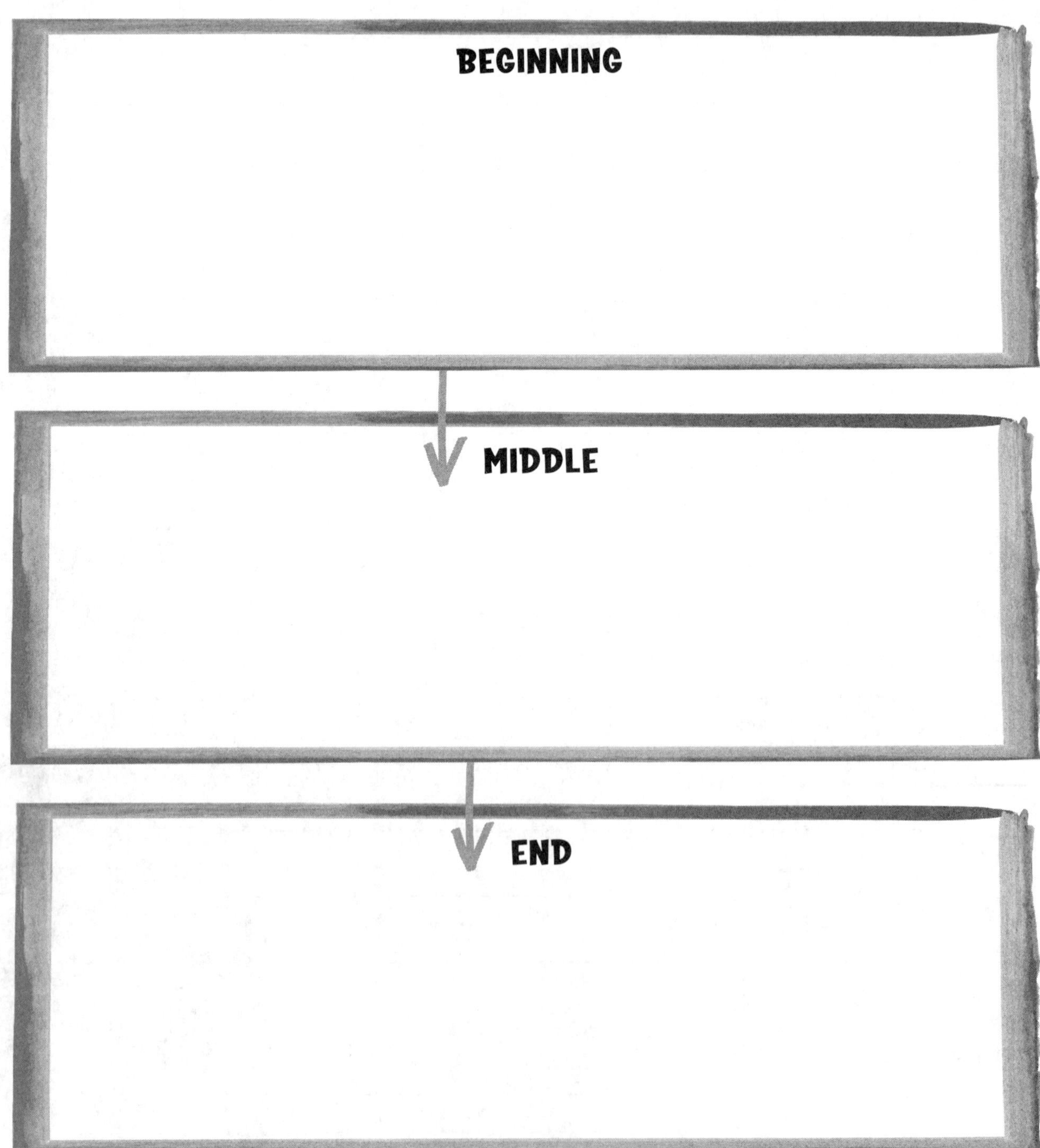

NAME: ______________________ **DATE:** ________________

Directions: Read the narrative paragraph about hiking at Yosemite. Then, answer the question.

Oliver woke up early because he was excited to go hiking at Yosemite. He gathered his backpack and made sure it had healthy snacks and his canteen. Right after breakfast, Oliver and his brother began their hike up the small peak by their campsite. At the top, they looked out over the beautiful land. On the way down, they looked for wildlife and saw a deer, a fox, and even a big bobcat in the distance. Stopping at a clear stream, Oliver refilled his canteen and splashed the cold water on his face. Though the brothers were tired from their hike, they ran back to their campsite to tell their parents about their fun day.

1. Describe one reason why this a good narrative draft.

____

____

____

Cursive Practice *abc*

Directions: Use cursive to write a sentence stating what you would like to do if you were to visit Yosemite National Park.

____

____

NAME: ____________________ **DATE:** ____________________

Directions: Read the sentences. Write two adjectives that could replace each underlined word.

1. They looked out over the <u>beautiful</u> land.

   ____________________ ____________________

2. Oliver saw a <u>big</u> bobcat in the distance.

   ____________________ ____________________

3. He splashed the <u>cold</u> water on his face.

   ____________________ ____________________

4. The brothers told their parents about their <u>fun</u> day.

   ____________________ ____________________

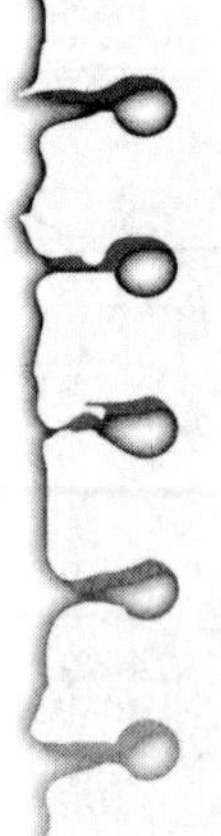

Boost Your Learning!

Not all adjectives are created equally! Some adjectives are **synonyms** and mean close to the same thing. Read how one word can make a difference.

- Nadia is a *nice* person.
- Nadia is a *friendly* person.
- Nadia is a *polite* person.

Make sure you choose adjectives that are interesting and specific.

NAME: ______________________ **DATE:** ________________

Editing
Yosemite

Directions: Each sentence is missing correct dialogue punctuation. Use the ∧ symbol to insert the quotation marks and comma for each sentence.

1. The sequoia trees are so tall said the hiker.

2. The tour guide said Yosemite was started in 1890.

3. I've never seen anything so beautiful said the visitor.

4. Dad said It's time for bed because we are hiking tomorrow.

5. Let's come again next year said the son.

Boost Your Learning!

Here are a few tips for using **quotation marks:**

- Quotation marks go before and after the words people say.
- The quote starts with a capital letter.
- If the quote comes before the person who said it, put a comma between the last word and ending quotation mark.

  Example: "Yosemite National Park is in California," the teacher explained.

- If the quote comes after the person who said it, put a comma between the person who spoke and the beginning quotation mark.

  Example: The boy said, "I would like to visit Yosemite someday."

NAME: ____________________ **DATE:** ____________________

Directions: Revisit the narrative about hiking. Add notes in the margins where dialogue could be added.

Oliver woke up early because he was excited to go hiking at Yosemite. He gathered his backpack and made sure it had healthy snacks and his canteen. Right after breakfast, Oliver and his brother began their hike up the small peak by their campsite. At the top, they looked out over the beautiful land. On the way down, they looked for wildlife and saw a deer, a fox, and even a big bobcat in the distance. Stopping at a clear stream, Oliver refilled his canteen and splashed the cold water on his face. Though the brothers were tired from their hike, they ran back to their campsite to tell their parents about their fun day.

This week I learned: 

- to include a beginning, a middle, and an end
- to choose specific adjectives
- to correctly use quotation marks and commas in dialogue

NAME: ______________________ **DATE:** ________________

Directions: Imagine two friends are going on a tour of the Grand Canyon on horses. Use the flowchart to write some ideas for the beginning, middle, and end of your narrative. Use your imagination as well as any information you may already know about the Grand Canyon to help you.

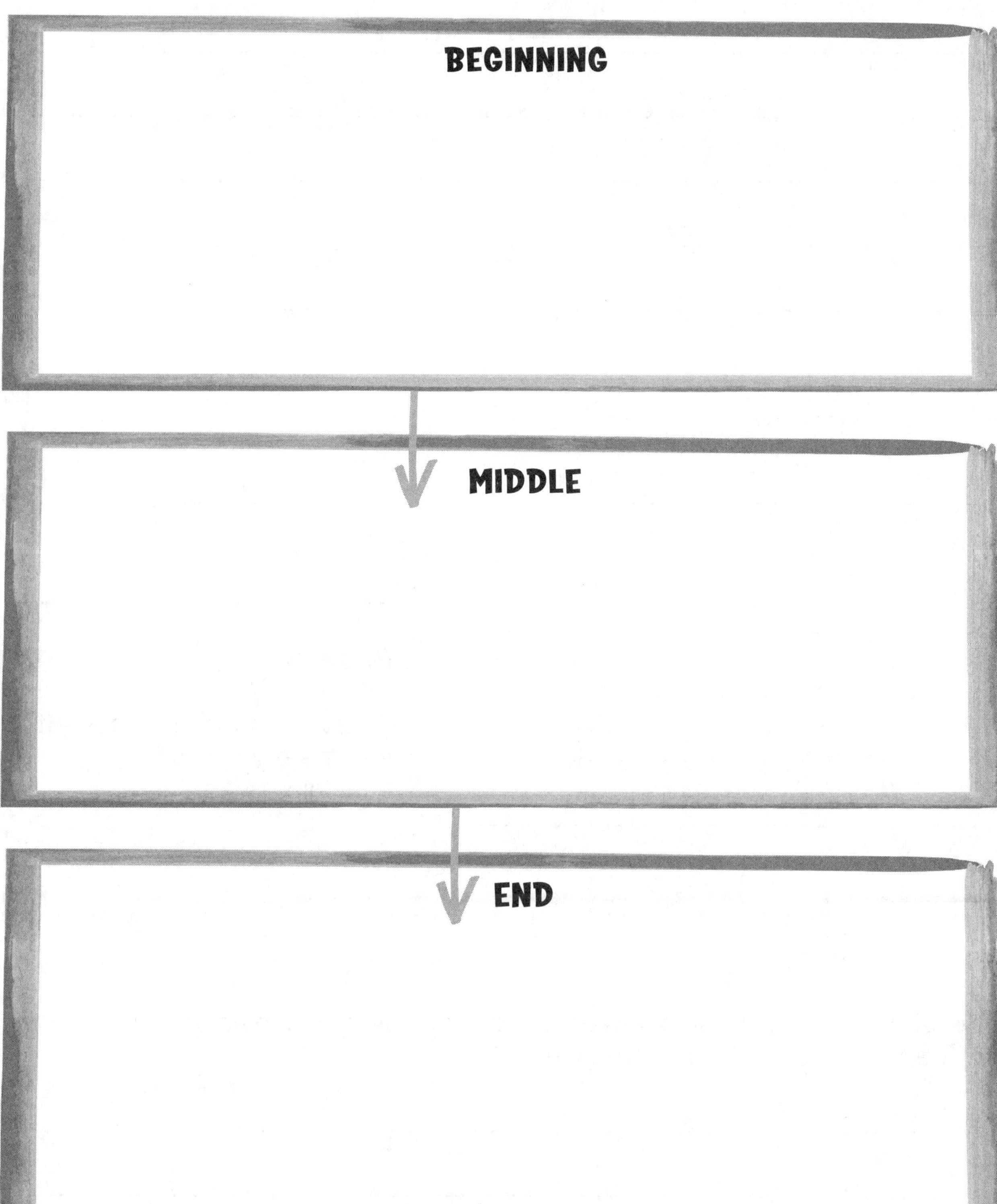

NAME: ______________________ **DATE:** ________________

Drafting
Grand Canyon

Directions: Imagine you are taking a tour of the Grand Canyon on horseback. Describe the experience, including details about how you feel and what the scenery looks like. Use your notes from page 79 to help you draft your narrative paragraph.

Remember!

A strong narrative paragraph tells a story with a beginning, a middle, and an end.

Cursive Practice

Directions: Use cursive to answer the following question: *Would you want to visit the Grand Canyon or the beach? Why?*

NAME: ____________________ **DATE:** ______________

Directions: Read the boring sentences. Make each one more exciting by adding adjectives.

Boring: My family and I went rafting in the Grand Canyon. **New and Improved:**
Boring: Everyone was scared except for me. **New and Improved:**
Boring: The water was rough. **New and Improved:**
Boring: One of the backpacks fell out of the raft. **New and Improved:**

Time to Improve! 

Reread the narrative paragraph you wrote on page 80. Do you have interesting, specific adjectives? Spice up your writing by adding some!

NAME: ______________________ **DATE:** ________________

Editing
Grand Canyon

Directions: Read each quotation Eli says to his mom. Then, write a response from his mom. Be sure to use correct punctuation. The first one is done for you.

1. Eli said, "I am looking forward to camping at the Grand Canyon."

   Mom said, "It will be fun to spend time with our family."

2. "I think going rafting on the water will be the best part!" exclaimed Eli.

   ____

   ____

3. Eli said, "I hope we see lots of wild animals."

   ____

   ____

4. "It's a bumpy, steep ride to the bottom of the canyon," cried Eli.

   ____

   ____

5. Eli shouted, "I can't believe how beautiful this place is!"

   ____

   ____

Time to Improve! 

Reread the paragraph you wrote on page 80 about the Grand Canyon. Make sure any dialogue uses quotation marks and commas correctly. If your paragraph does not have any dialogue, add at least one line.

NAME: ______________________ **DATE:** ______________

Directions: Imagine you are taking a tour of the Grand Canyon on horseback. Describe the experience, including details about how you feel and what the scenery looks like.

NAME: ______________________________ **DATE:** ____________________

Directions: Read through the notes below. Place check marks by five to seven things you think should be included in a personal narrative paragraph about four square.

_____ I played on Wednesday when it was windy.

_____ Nick wanted to swing instead.

_____ Marco kept catching the ball.

_____ Meg kicked the ball by accident.

_____ The recess teachers were watching the soccer field.

_____ Marco argued about the ball hitting the line.

_____ Lauren was alone, so we invited her to join us.

_____ Girls were jump roping close by.

_____ I never got out.

NAME: ______________________ **DATE:** ______________

Directions: Read the narrative paragraph about playing four square. Some of the sentences are not in order. Order the middle sentences from 1 to 5 in an order that makes sense to you.

Last Wednesday, some friends and I had fun playing four square during recess. _____Marco kept catching the ball, and we had to remind him to only hit it. _____Once Meg got confused and kicked the ball, which was really funny. _____A girl was standing by herself, not playing with anyone, so we invited her to join us. _____Marco also argued with us about the ball hitting the line when he served. _____The best part of playing was that I did not get out one time. Playing four square was really fun!

Cursive Practice

Directions: Use cursive to write one thing you like about four square.

____

____

NAME: ______________________ **DATE:** ________________

Directions: Read each sentence. Shade in the circle with the correct synonym for each underlined word. Then, write your own synonym pair.

1. Four square is <u>fun</u>!
   Ⓐ entertaining
   Ⓑ complicated
   Ⓒ easy

2. Players can <u>hit</u> the ball with their hands.
   Ⓐ swat
   Ⓑ catch
   Ⓒ rub

3. The rules are <u>flexible</u>.
   Ⓐ difficult
   Ⓑ simple
   Ⓒ changeable

4. The game has simple <u>equipment</u>.
   Ⓐ winners
   Ⓑ gear
   Ⓒ instructions

5. ______________________ ______________________

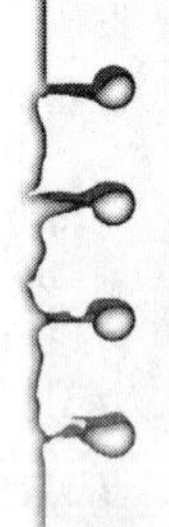

Boost Your Learning! 

Synonyms are words that mean the same (or close to the same) thing.

Examples: *big* and *huge*, *small* and *tiny*, *mug* and *cup*

NAME: ______________________ **DATE:** ______________

Directions: Use the words in the Word Bank to write the missing relative pronouns in the sentences.

1. Ms. Grey, ______________ the school hired, is a great P.E. teacher.
2. Cherise prefers playing with a ball ______________ she brought from home.
3. Caleb, ______________ is a great player, is always chosen first.
4. Terry, ______________ playing isn't the best, always blames the server.
5. The playground, ______________ is paved, is a great place to play.

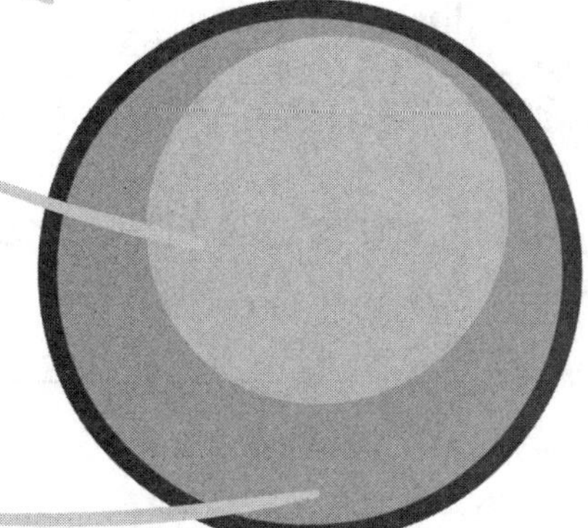

Boost Your Learning!

A **pronoun** is a word that takes the place of a noun.

Examples: *he*, *she*, *it*, and *they*

Words like those used in this activity are called **relative pronouns**.

NAME: ______________________ **DATE:** ______________

Publishing
Four Square

Directions: Read the paragraph. Then, answer the questions.

Last Wednesday, some friends and I had fun playing four square during recess. A girl was standing by herself, not playing with anyone, so we invited her to join us. Marco kept catching the ball, and we had to remind him to only hit it. Marco also argued with us about the ball hitting the line when he served. Once Meg got confused and kicked the ball, which was really funny. The best part of playing was that I did not get out one time. Playing four square was really entertaining!

This week I learned: 

- to include relevant information
- to organize my ideas
- to use interesting adjectives

1. Discuss two strengths about the paragraph.

____

____

____

2. What advice would you give the author to improve the paragraph?

____

____

____

NAME: ______________________ **DATE:** ________________

Directions: Think of a time you played kickball. Write your thoughts about that game in the right column. If you have not played kickball, use your imagination to write your notes. Then, put stars by four to six ideas you would like to include in a personal narrative paragraph about playing kickball.

NAME: ______________________ **DATE:** ________________

Directions: Write about a time when you played kickball. Describe the experience, including details about whom you played with and how the game went. Use the notes from page 89 to help you draft your personal narrative paragraph.

Remember!

A strong personal narrative:

- is about you
- has a beginning, a middle, and an end
- sounds like a story

Cursive Practice

Directions: Use cursive to write one kickball rule.

NAME: ______________________________ **DATE:** ____________________

Directions: Write three adjectives for each noun in the table. Then, use some of your adjectives to improve the sentences below.

Today's Weather	A Kickball	Student

1. The student kicked the kickball during recess.

____

____

2. The kickball sailed over the student's head.

____

____

3. The weather couldn't stop the student from playing.

____

____

Time to Improve! 

Revisit the personal narrative paragraph you wrote on page 90 about kickball. Have you used any adjectives? If not, add some to make your writing more exciting!

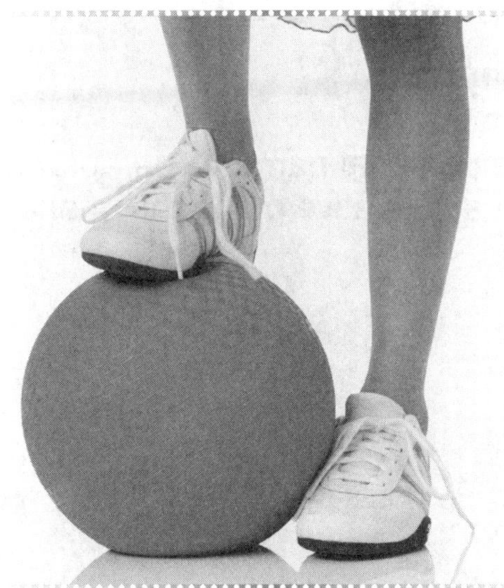

NAME: ____________________________ **DATE:** ____________________

Directions: Read the paragraph about kickball. The underlined pronouns are not correct. Use the ⅇ symbol to delete the incorrect words. Then, use the ∧ symbol to insert the correct words from the Relative Pronoun Bank. **Note:** You may use a relative pronoun more than once.

Relative Pronoun Bank			
whom	whose	which	that

Though invented in the early 1900s, kickball is a game <u>whose</u> began gaining popularity with school-aged children in the 1970s. The field, <u>who</u> is similar to baseball, has three bases, home plate, a pitcher's area, and an outfield. Nicholas C. Seuss, <u>that</u> the kickball was invented by, wrote a book of playground games in 1917 and called the new sport "Kick Baseball." Daniel Chase, <u>which</u> the New York State Board of Education hired, wrote about the first known adult kickball game in 1922. Children, <u>whom</u> resources are sometimes limited, can easily play in an open field with just a ball. Today, children can be seen playing kickball on almost every playground at recess.

Time to Improve! 

Reread the personal narrative paragraph you wrote on page 90 about kickball. If you have any relative pronouns, make sure they are used correctly.

NAME: ______________________ **DATE:** ________________

Directions: Write about a time when you played kickball. Describe the experience, including details about whom you played with and how the game went.

NAME: ____________________ **DATE:** ____________________

Directions: Place check marks in the circles that belong in an informative/explanatory paragraph about Wilbur and Orville Wright's first flight.

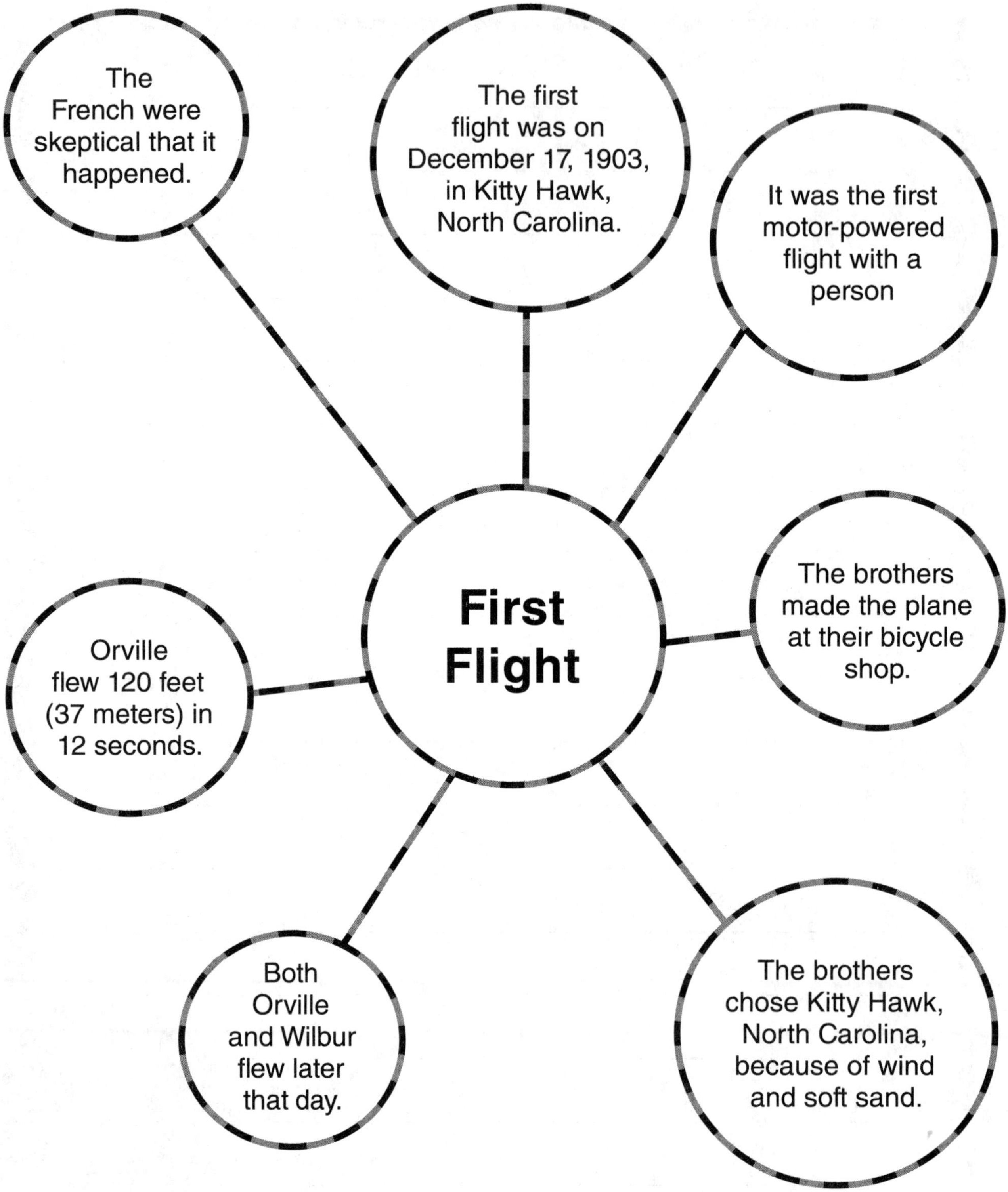

First Flight

- The French were skeptical that it happened.
- The first flight was on December 17, 1903, in Kitty Hawk, North Carolina.
- It was the first motor-powered flight with a person
- The brothers made the plane at their bicycle shop.
- The brothers chose Kitty Hawk, North Carolina, because of wind and soft sand.
- Both Orville and Wilbur flew later that day.
- Orville flew 120 feet (37 meters) in 12 seconds.

NAME: ____________________ **DATE:** ______________

Directions: Read the informative/explanatory paragraph about the Wright brothers' first flight. Then, answer the question.

The Wright brothers made history and accomplished a life-long dream when they flew for the first time. The historic flight happened on December 17, 1903, in Kitty Hawk, North Carolina. When the French heard, they were skeptical the flight actually happened. Kitty Hawk was windy, which would help with the flight, and had a sandy beach, which would be good in case of a crash. Orville was the first pilot and flew 120 feet (37 meters) in 12 seconds. The plane was more like a motorized glider. That day, each brother took turns flying. It was a day that carved the path for modern flight.

1. Cross out one sentence you think should be taken out. Explain why it should be deleted.

____

____

____

Cursive Practice *abc*

Directions: Use cursive to write *Orville and Wilbur Wright, first in flight*.

____

____

NAME: ______________________ **DATE:** ________________

Directions: Read each sentence. Write the correct plural form of each irregular noun on the line.

1. The first flight went 120 ______________ (foot) .
2. Neither Orville nor Wilbur married or had ______________ (child) .
3. Thousands of ______________ (person) fly on airplanes every day.
4. There may have been ______________ (goose) at the Kitty Hawk beach.
5. Some ______________ (mouse) scurried around the beach.
6. Many ______________ (woman) and their families witnessed this first flight.

Boost Your Learning!

Usually, to make a noun plural, you just add *-s*.

Example: airplane ➔ airplanes

Some nouns are **irregular** and do not follow a rule.

Example: child ➔ children

NAME: ______________________ **DATE:** ______________

Directions: Read the sentences. Use the ≡ symbol to show which words should be capitalized. Then, write why the words need to be capitalized.

1. the wright brothers made history and accomplished a life-long dream.

   ____

   ____

2. the historic flight happened on december 17, 1903, in kitty hawk, north carolina.

   ____

   ____

3. orville and wilbur were from ohio, but went to north carolina for the flight.

   ____

   ____

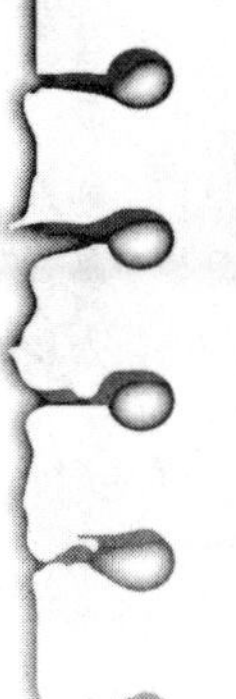

Boost Your Learning!

Proper nouns name specific people, places, and things. They should always be capitalized. Use the ≡ symbol to show when a lowercase letter should be capitalized.

Example: The Wright Brothers' plane is in the smithsonian museum.

NAME: ______________________ **DATE:** ______________

Directions: Think about what you practiced this week. In the margins, make a list of at least three things you would do to improve the paragraph.

The wright brothers made history and accomplished a life-long dream when they flew for the first time. The historic flight happened on december 17, 1903, in kitty hawk, north carolina. When the french heard, they were skeptical the flight actually happened. Kitty hawk was windy, which would help with the flight, and had a sandy beach, which would be good in case of a crash. Orville was the first pilot and flew 120 feet (37 meters) in 12 seconds. The plane was more like a motorized glider. That day, each brother took turns flying. It was a day that carved the path for modern flight.

This week I learned: 

- to include supporting details
- to capitalize proper nouns
- to make irregular nouns plural

NAME: ______________________________ **DATE:** ____________________

Directions: This web focuses on the production of Henry Ford's car, the Model-T. Place check marks in the parts of the web that should be included in an informative/explanatory paragraph.

Production of the Model-T

- It was made with interchangeable parts, so the car took less time to make.
- Workers were paid $5.00 a day; most other workers were paid $2.34 a day.
- Ford's son, Edsel, took over the company in 1919.
- It was introduced in October 1908.
- It was nicknamed the "Tin Lizzie."
- Ford did not invent the car or assembly line.
- It was made on a moving assembly line, so the car was less expensive to make.

NAME: ____________________ **DATE:** ____________________

Directions: Write about the production of Henry Ford's Model-T car. Include facts about the Model-T and the employees who helped make the cars. Use the information on page 99 to help you draft your informative/explanatory paragraph.

Remember!

A strong informative/explanatory paragraph includes:

- introductory and concluding sentences
- details which support the main idea

Cursive Practice

Directions: Use cursive to write these names: *Henry Ford*, *Model-T*, and *Tin Lizzie*.

NAME: ______________________ **DATE:** ________________

Directions: Read the paragraph with missing words. Use the plural form of the words in the Word Bank to fill in the blanks.

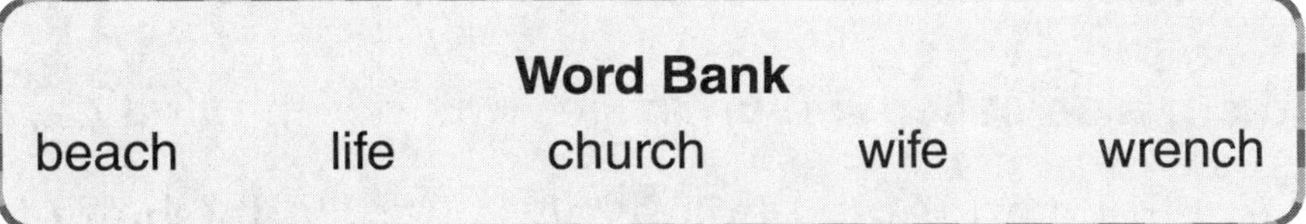

As the Model-T became more popular, people's ______________ began to change. Suddenly, cars were parked in front of ______________ and along sandy ______________. Husbands tinkered under the hoods with ______________, while ______________ wanted driving lessons. Traveling would never be the same.

Boost Your Learning!

If a noun ends in an *-f*, change the *-f* to *-v* and add *-es*.

Example: *elf* ➔ *elves*

If a noun ends in **-*ch***, add *-es*.

Example: *branch* ➔ *branches*

Time to Improve!

Look at the paragraph you wrote on page 100 for any plural nouns. If they are irregular, pay special attention that they are correct.

NAME: ____________________ **DATE:** ____________

Directions: Read the paragraph about the Model-T. Correct any capitalization errors using the ≡ or / symbols.

The model-t, also called the tin lizzie, was not the first car invented, but it was very Popular! At the height of its popularity, half of the Cars in America were the model-T. It came in only one color—Black—and henry ford joked that customers could have the car in any color they wanted, as long as it was black. He also placed the Steering Wheel on the left side, which became standard in america. The tin lizzie was a pioneer in the Auto World.

Remember! 

Use the correct symbols to show words that should be capital or lowercase.

Time to Improve! 

Carefully reread the paragraph you wrote on page 100 about the Model-T. Make sure all proper nouns are capitalized.

NAME: ____________________ **DATE:** ____________________

Directions: Write about the production of Henry Ford's Model-T car. Include facts about the Model-T and the employees who helped make the cars.

NAME: ______________________ **DATE:** ______________

Directions: Read the narrative notes in the flowchart. Put stars by six to eight things you think should be in a narrative paragraph about a boy learning to snowboard.

BEGINNING

_____ new to Utah and saw snowboarding for the first time

_____ wanted to learn

_____ seemed really hard

MIDDLE

_____ talked to his mom about getting equipment

_____ read online articles about terms

_____ oldest in beginner's class

_____ fell down a lot

_____ wanted to give up

END

_____ clean run down the mountain

_____ made new friends

_____ amazing feeling of accomplishment

NAME: ______________________ **DATE:** ______________

Directions: Read the narrative paragraph about Dante's snowboarding experience. Underline sentences that you think are interesting and add to the story.

When Dante moved to Utah, he saw snowboarders for the first time. He immediately wanted to learn. He asked his mom about equipment.

"That stuff is expensive!" she exclaimed, but she let him take lessons. As the oldest in his beginner's class, he sometimes felt embarrassed, but he never gave up. He made new friends. He fell down over and over, and each time he felt like he was at the beginning. Dante read articles online to learn the different terms and studied different moves. Most of all, he wanted to do a flip. Between lessons and studying, he was working very hard. After several lessons, he finally had a clean run down the mountain.

"This is awesome!" he yelled as he enjoyed his amazing accomplishment.

Cursive Practice *abc*

Directions: Use cursive to write one question you have about snowboarding.

____

____

NAME: ______________________ **DATE:** ______________

Directions: Read the sentences. Write an idiom from the Idiom Bank that could replace the underlined words in each one.

Idiom Bank		
costs an arm and a leg	back to square one	best of both worlds

1. He fell down over and over, and each time he felt like he was <u>at the beginning</u>.

   ____

2. That stuff <u>is expensive</u> she exclaimed.

   ____

3. Since he loves the snow and loves being active, snowboarding has <u>all of the advantages</u>.

   ____

Boost Your Learning!

An **idiom** is an expression that cannot be understood literally. Its meaning is something different.

Example: The answer was on the <u>tip of his tongue</u>. This means he knows the answer, but cannot think of it at that moment.

NAME: ____________________ **DATE:** ________________

Directions: Add punctuation to the dialogue.

1. That stuff is expensive she exclaimed
2. Samuel asked Where is my snowboard
3. This is awesome he yelled
4. May I borrow your goggles today Ella asked her brother
5. Most of all he wanted to do a flip Ella said

Boost Your Learning!

When a quotation is an exclamation or a question, put an exclamation point or a question mark at the end of what is said but before the final quotation mark.

Examples

"Watch out!" James yelled.

Dad asked, "What time are you coming home?"

NAME: ______________________ **DATE:** ________________

Directions: Reread the narrative paragraph. Think about what you have learned this week. Write at least three suggestions for how to improve the paragraph on the lines below.

When Dante moved to Utah, he saw snowboarders for the first time. He immediately wanted to learn. He asked his mom about equipment. That stuff is expensive she exclaimed, but she let him take lessons. As the oldest in his beginner's class, he sometimes felt embarrassed, but he never gave up. He made new friends. He fell down over and over, and each time he felt like he was at the beginning. Dante read articles online to learn the different terms and studied different moves. Most of all, he wanted to do a flip. Between lessons and studying, he was working very hard. After several lessons, he finally had a clean run down the mountain. This is awesome he yelled as he enjoyed his amazing accomplishment.

____

____

____

____

____

____

____

____

____

____

This week I learned: 

- to write a narrative with a beginning, a middle, and an end
- to use idioms
- to correctly use quotation marks

NAME: ______________________ **DATE:** ________________

Directions: Use the flowchart to write ideas for a narrative paragraph about a fourth grader going ice skating for the first time. You can use your imagination or events from your own experiences.

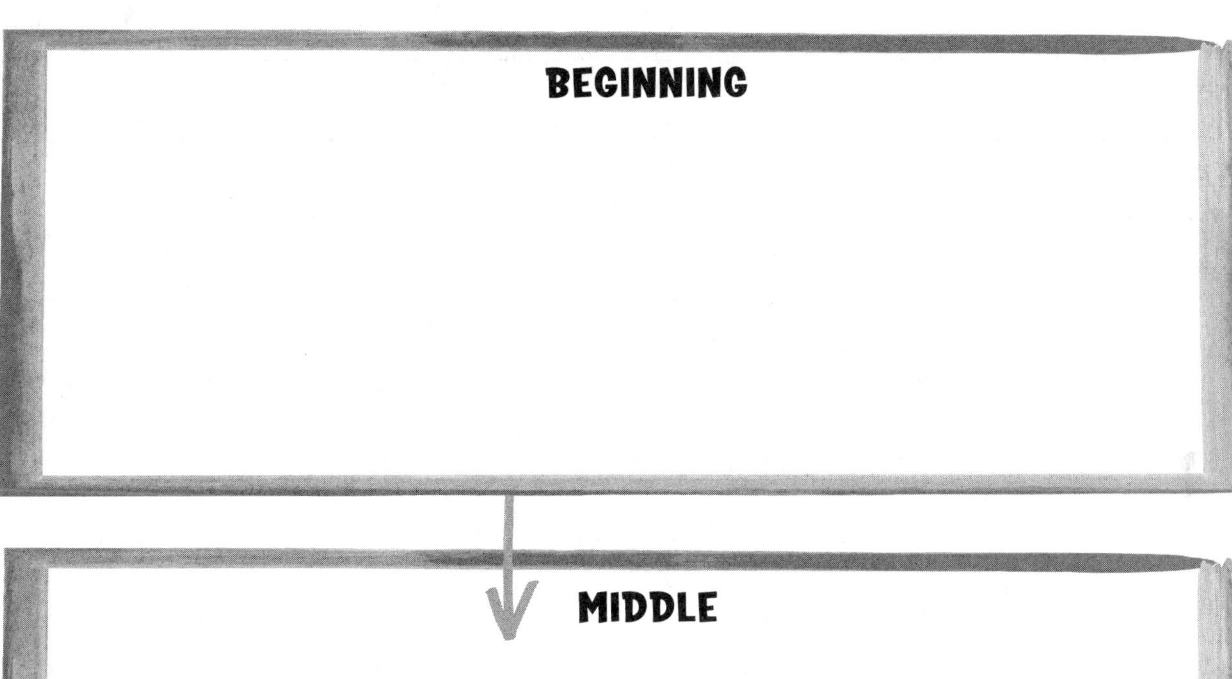

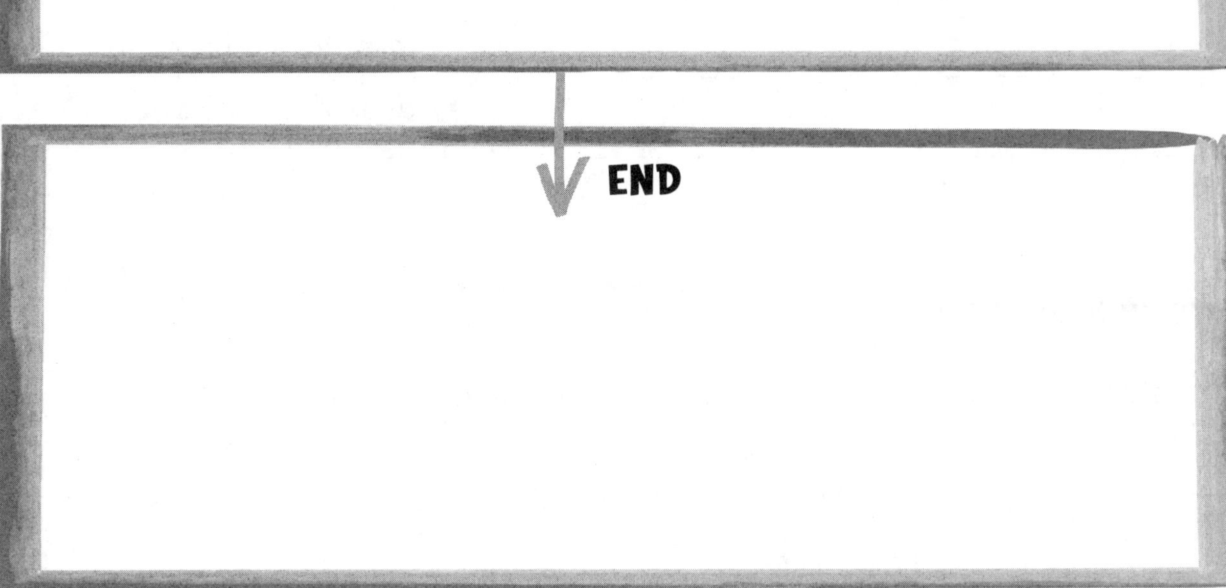

NAME: ______________________ **DATE:** ________________

Directions: Describe a time when a fourth grader goes ice skating for the first time. Include details of the experience and how the character felt. Use your notes from page 109 to help you draft your narrative paragraph.

Remember!

A strong narrative paragraph:

- has a beginning, a middle, and an end
- tells events in order
- uses dialogue and descriptions

Cursive Practice

Directions: Use cursive to write two things you like about ice skating.

NAME: ______________________ **DATE:** ______________

Directions: Write the correct letter to match each idiom with its meaning. Then, choose two idioms from the list, and write one sentence for each idiom.

_____ 1. to sound familiar

_____ 2. to do immediately without warning

_____ 3. ignoring someone

_____ 4. always together

_____ 5. worry about something that is not a big deal

A. cold shoulder

B. ring a bell

C. joined at the hip

D. split hairs

E. at the drop of a hat

6. ____

____

7. ____

____

Time to Improve! 

Idioms can be fun to use when writing! Look over the paragraph you wrote on page 110 to see if there is room for one in your narrative.

NAME: ______________________ **DATE:** ________________

Directions: Use the ≡ and ∧ symbols to correct the dialogue.

1. "falling down hurts!" exclaimed Jess.

2. "When are we leaving for the rink," asked Edward?

3. Sierra said, "black ice skates are my favorite."

4. Jeremiah asked "Are we going to be late for practice?"

5. "I love gliding along the ice" stated Rachael.

Time to Improve! 

Look back at the paragraph you wrote on page 110. Do you have any dialogue? If you do, make sure it has correct punctuation. If you do not, consider adding some!

Remember! 

If a line of dialogue is a question or exclamation, put the quotation mark after the question mark or exclamation point.

NAME: ______________________ **DATE:** ______________

Directions: Describe a time when a fourth grader goes ice skating for the first time. Include details of the experience and how the character felt.

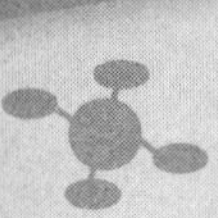

NAME: ______________________ **DATE:** ________________

Directions: Mozart was a composer from the 1700s who wrote symphonies. He was a musical genius and performed for royalty at the age of five. Think about this question: *Should Mozart have been required to perform at such a young age?* If an idea below supports the "yes" argument, write *Y*. If it supports the "no" argument, write *N*.

_____ 1. He should share his gift with others.

_____ 2. He was too young.

_____ 3. There were other talented people to perform.

_____ 4. Performing is too much pressure.

_____ 5. People did what royalty said to do.

_____ 6. Playing for royalty could make him famous.

NAME: ______________________________ **DATE:** ____________________

Directions: Read the opinion paragraph. It argues that Mozart should have been required to perform for royalty. Underline parts that support this opinion.

Mozart was a musical genius whose father made the right decision to let Mozart play for royalty at age five. This child had an amazing gift, and it needed to be shared with others. In Mozart's day, people had to do what royalty said. He or his family could have suffered severe consequences if they refused. Performing for royalty was too much pressure on such a small child. There were older musicians who could have performed for royalty. Though Mozart was young, performing was the right thing for him.

Cursive Practice

Directions: Mozart's full name was quite long, so he generally went by Wolfgang Amadeus Mozart. Use cursive to write his full name.

____

____

NAME: ______________________ **DATE:** ________________

Directions: Rewrite the sentences by replacing the underlined words with the base words and the prefixes *re-*, *mis-*, or *pre-* and deleting the words in bold. The first one has been done for you.

1. The pianist has to try the complicated music **again**.

   The pianist has to retry the complicated music.

2. Some people think Mozart was treated **wrongly** as a child.

   ____

   ____

3. Musicians often view the music **before** they play.

   ____

   ____

4. Sarah discovered her love of classical music **again**.

   ____

   ____

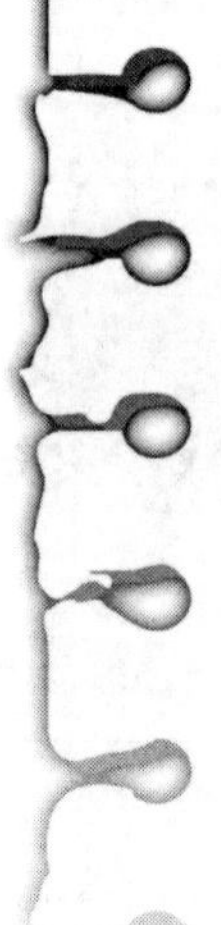

Boost Your Learning!

A **prefix** is a group of letters added to the beginning of a base word, which changes the base word's meaning.

Examples

- *re-* means "again"
- *mis-* means "wrong"
- *pre-* means "before"

NAME: ______________________ **DATE:** ________________

Directions: Use the  symbol to correct the spelling of the prepositions.

1. Mozart puts his violin insde the case.

2. He sets the case onn the seat.

3. He is led nito the beautiful room.

4. Walking arcoss the grand hall, Mozart prepares to play.

5. The king nods toeward Mozart.

6. He places the violin undr his chin.

7. He takes a deep breath bfore the music starts.

8. The royals applaud aftr his performance.

Boost Your Learning!

A **preposition** is a word that describes the relationship between two nouns.

Examples: *above*, *before*, *in*, *near*, *over*, *through*, *under*

NAME: ______________________ **DATE:** ______________

Directions: Read the paragraph. Then, answer the question.

Mozart was a musical genius whose father made the right decision to let Mozart play for royalty at age five. This child had an amazing gift, and it needed to be shared with others. In Mozart's day, people had to do what royalty said. He or his family could have suffered severe consequences if they refused. Performing for royalty may have put too much pressure on such a small child. There were older musicians who could have performed for royalty. Though Mozart was young, performing was the right thing for him.

This week I learned: 

- to use details and information to support my opinion
- about the prefixes *pre-*, *re-*, and *mis-*
- about prepositions

1. What advice would you give to the author to improve this paragraph?

____

____

____

____

NAME: ______________________ **DATE:** ______________

Directions: Read the information about Beethoven. Then, answer the question below by filling in the table.

Beethoven was a musician and composer who lived from 1770 to 1827. He composed nine symphonies and dozens of pieces of music for the piano and string quartets. Beethoven was completely deaf when he composed his most important works. Students from elementary school to college study his music.

Should Beethoven's classical music still be taught today?

Yes	No

NAME: ______________________ **DATE:** ______________

Directions: Should Beethoven's classical music still be taught today? Explain why you think Beethoven's music should or should not be taught today. Use your notes from page 119 to help you draft your opinion paragraph.

Remember!

A strong opinion paragraph includes:

- an introductory sentence stating your opinion
- details that support your opinion
- a concluding sentence that restates your opinion

Cursive Practice

Directions: Use cursive to write the following: *Ludwig van Beethoven*, *symphony*, *quartet*

NAME: ____________________ **DATE:** ______________

Directions: Complete each sentence with a prefix from the Prefix Bank. Then, use one of the prefixes to create your own sentence.

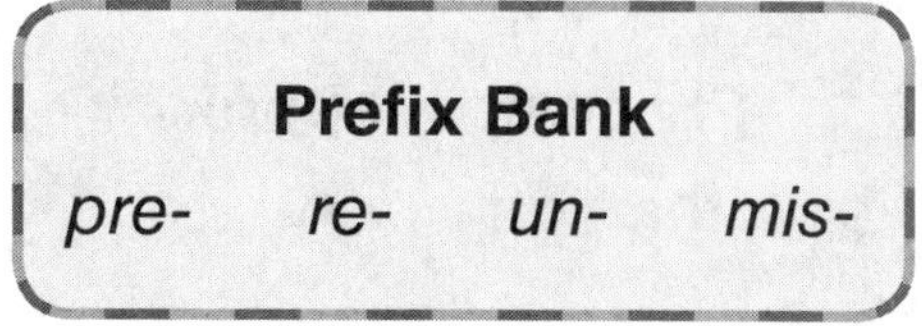

Prefix Bank

pre- *re-* *un-* *mis-*

1. Mozart _____dates Beethoven by only 14 years.
2. Beethoven was performing concertos while children today at his age are in _____school.
3. It was _____fortunate that Beethoven went deaf, but he did not let it stop him.
4. Beethoven _____visited sections of music when composing.
5. There may have been times where Beethoven _____understood the notes.
6. ____

____

Remember! 

The prefixes *pre*-, *re*-, *un*-, and *mis*- have their own meanings.

- *re*- means "again"
- *mis*- means "wrong"
- *pre*- means "before"
- *un*- means "not"

Time to Improve! 

Look at the opinion paragraph you wrote on page 120 for words with prefixes. Do you have any *pre*-, *re*-, *un*-, or *mis*- words? If so, make sure they are used correctly!

NAME: ____________________ **DATE:** ____________________

Directions: The paragraph is missing some prepositions. Use the ∧ symbol to insert the prepositions from the Preposition Bank.

Preposition Bank

in   to   through   on   of   near

When Beethoven was only 26 years old, he began to have a "ringing" __________ his ears. This was the beginning __________ Beethoven's hearing loss. By age 31, his doctor recommended he spend time in a small town __________ Vienna, Austria, so he could get used __________ his condition. He was depressed, but vowed to work __________ it and not give up __________ music. Gradually, he became profoundly deaf. He could not play music, but he could still compose.

Remember! 

Prepositions show the relationship between two nouns.

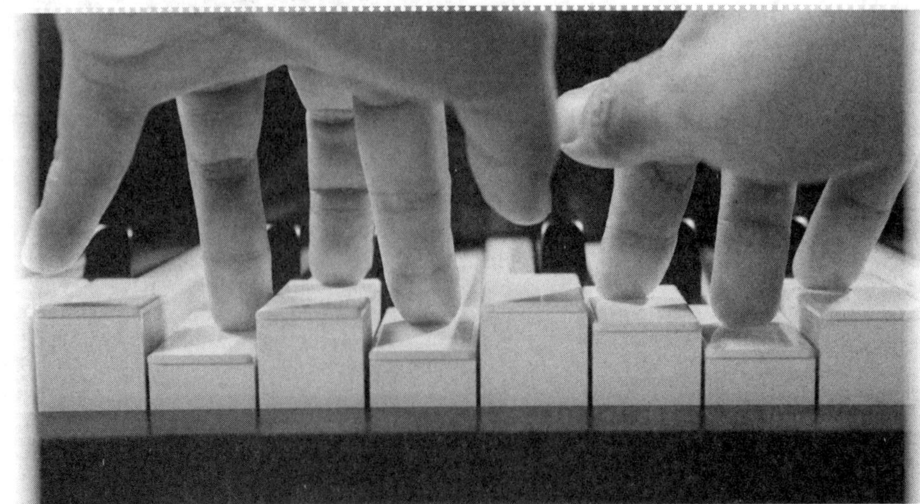

NAME: ______________________________ **DATE:** ____________________

Directions: Should Beethoven's classical music still be taught today? Explain why you think Beethoven's music should or should not be taught today.

NAME: ______________________ DATE: ______________

Directions: Read the information in the web. The notes are for an informative/explanatory paragraph focusing on the asteroid belt. Place check marks in the circles with information that supports the main topic.

Asteroid Belt

- An asteroid hitting Earth might have caused the dinosaurs' extinction.
- Billions or trillions of asteroids are in the asteroid belt.
- Sizes range from a pebble to over 150 miles (241 kilometers) in diameter.
- The dwarf planet Ceres is part of the asteroid belt.
- A small asteroid hit Russia in 2013.
- The asteroids are 600,000 miles (965,606 kilometers) apart.
- Movies have been made about asteroids hitting Earth.
- Most of the asteroids are lumpy.

NAME: ______________________ **DATE:** ________________

Directions: Read the draft of an informative/explanatory paragraph about the asteroid belt. Underline the incomplete sentences.

Between Mars and Jupiter, there is an asteroid belt. Billions—perhaps trillions—of asteroids orbit the sun. Small pebbles to 150 miles (241 kilometers) diameter. The largest asteroid is actually a dwarf planet named Ceres. Asteroids 600,000 miles (965,606 kilometers) apart. This distance is more than 24 Earths, so there is little danger of a spacecraft hitting one while on a mission. Lumpy not round. This is because asteroids do not have enough gravity to pull the particles into a sphere. Scientists are still learning about the asteroid belt.

Cursive Practice *abc*

Directions: Use cursive to write one question you have about the asteroid belt.

____

____

NAME: ______________________ **DATE:** ________________

Revising
Asteroids

Directions: Read the sentences. Circle the subject and underline the predicate in each one. The first one is done for you.

1. The dwarf planet Ceres is an asteroid in the asteroid belt.

2. Ceres was discovered in 1801 by Giuseppe Piazzi.

3. The asteroid is about one-fourth the size of Earth's moon.

4. The Herschel Space Observatory discovered water vapor on Ceres.

5. A year on Ceres is equal to 4.6 Earth years.

Directions: Create your own sentence about asteroids. Then, circle the subject and underline the predicate.

6. ____

____

Remember! 

Every sentence must have a:

- subject (who or what the sentence is about)
- predicate (verb and what happens in the sentence)

NAME: ______________________ **DATE:** ______________

Directions: Read the dictionary definitions of *dwarf*. Then, answer the questions below.

dwarf \dwôrf\

1. *noun.* a mythical creature that looks like a small man
2. *noun.* a person who is smaller than normal because of a medical condition
3. *verb.* to make something seem much smaller by comparison
4. *adjective.* smaller than usual

1. Read this sentence: *The largest asteroid is actually a dwarf planet.* Which definition of the word *dwarf* is being used in this sentence? How do you know?

____

____

2. Read this sentence: *Small pebble asteroids are dwarfed by the sun.* Which definition of *dwarf* is being used in this sentence? How do you know?

____

____

3. Write a sentence using a definition of *dwarf* that has not been used yet.

____

____

NAME: ______________________ **DATE:** ________________

Publishing

Asteroids

Directions: Read the paragraph. Then, answer the question.

Between Mars and Jupiter, there is an asteroid belt. Billions—perhaps trillions—of asteroids orbit the sun. Small pebbles to 150 miles (241 kilometers) diameter. The largest asteroid is actually a dwarf planet named Ceres. Asteroids 600,000 miles (965,606 kilometers) apart. This distance is more than 24 Earths, so there is little danger of a spacecraft hitting one while on a mission. Lumpy not round. This is because asteroids do not have enough gravity to pull the particles into a sphere. Scientists are still learning about the asteroid belt.

This week I learned:

- to include strong details
- to write sentences with subjects and predicates
- to use word entries in dictionaries

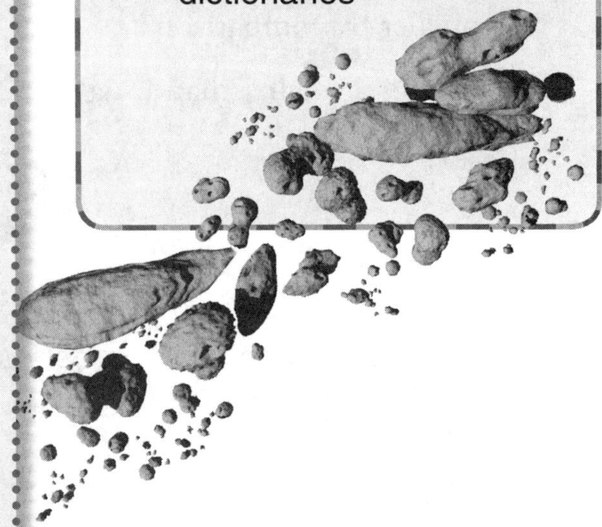

1. How could the author have improved this published paragraph?

____

____

____

____

____

NAME: ______________________ **DATE:** ________________

Directions: Read the information. The notes are for an informative/explanatory paragraph about what comets look like. Place check marks in the circles with information that supports the main topic.

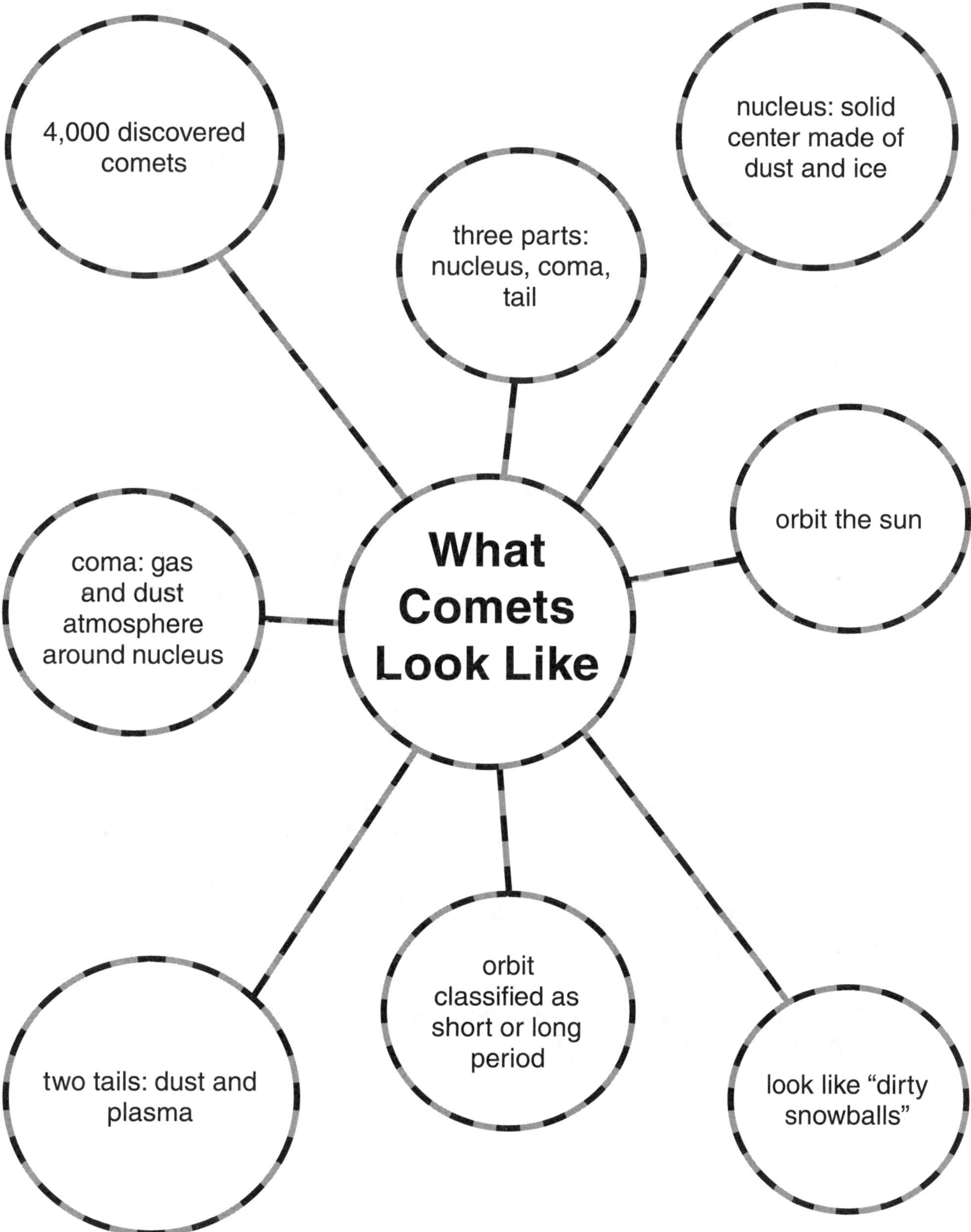

NAME: ______________________ **DATE:** ______________

Directions: Write about what a comet looks like. Include facts that tell about the parts of a comet. Use the web from page 129 to help you draft your informative/explanatory paragraph.

Remember!

A strong informative/explanatory paragraph includes:

- an introductory and a concluding sentence
- details that support the main idea
- complete sentences

Cursive Practice

Directions: Use cursive to write the names of these famous comets: *Halley's*, *Lovejoy*, *Hale-Bopp*, and *McNaught*.

NAME: ______________________ **DATE:** ________________

Directions: Read each phrase about Halley's Comet. Rewrite the fragments into complete sentences with subjects and predicates.

1. named for Edmond Halley

____

____

2. appears 75 years

____

____

3. oldest record 240 B.C.E. in China

____

____

4. shaped like peanut

____

____

Time to Improve! 

Reread the paragraph you wrote on page 130 about comets. Make sure each sentence has a subject and a predicate. If you find a fragment or a run-on sentence, fix it!

Editing
Comets

NAME: ______________________ **DATE:** ______________

Directions: Read the dictionary definitions for the word *period*. Then, answer the questions below.

period \pirēəd\

1. *noun.* a dot used to show the end of a sentence when writing
2. *noun.* a length of time during which an event takes place
3. *noun.* one of the parts a game is divided into

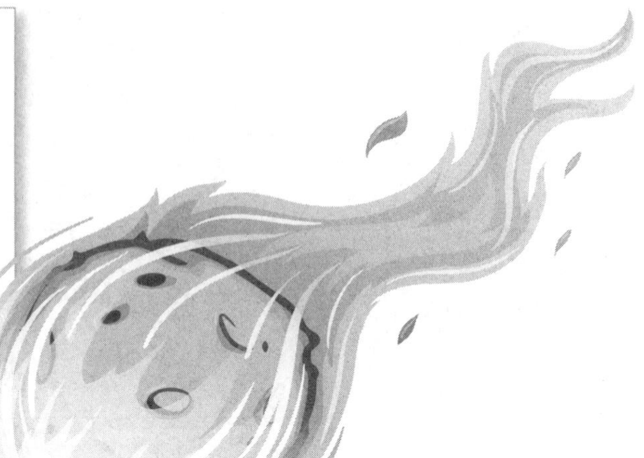

1. Read this sentence: *A short period comet has an orbit of less than 200 years.* What definition of *period* is being used in this sentence? _____

2. Read this sentence: *The score was tied after the first period.* What definition of *period* is being used in this sentence? _____

3. Write your own sentence using the first definition of *period*.

____

____

Remember!

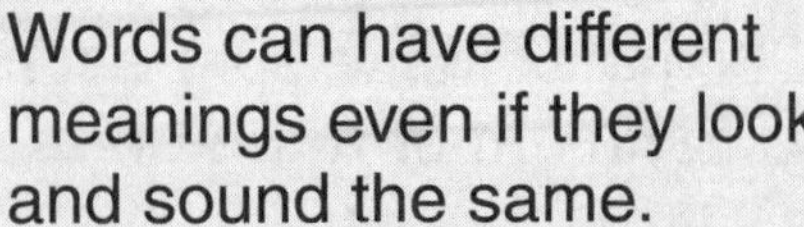

Words can have different meanings even if they look and sound the same.

Time to Improve! 

Look at the paragraph you wrote on page 130 and check that the vocabulary words are being used correctly.

NAME: ______________________ **DATE:** ________________

Directions: Write about what a comet looks like. Include facts that tell about the parts of a comet.

NAME: ______________________________ **DATE:** ____________________

Directions: Read the notes about using solar energy. Decide if each note is an advantage or a disadvantage and write it in the table.

- cannot collect energy at night or on cloudy days
- expensive to install
- does not produce pollution
- once built, has low operating cost
- is a clean, renewable resource
- not very efficient at changing energy to electricity
- costs coming down over time

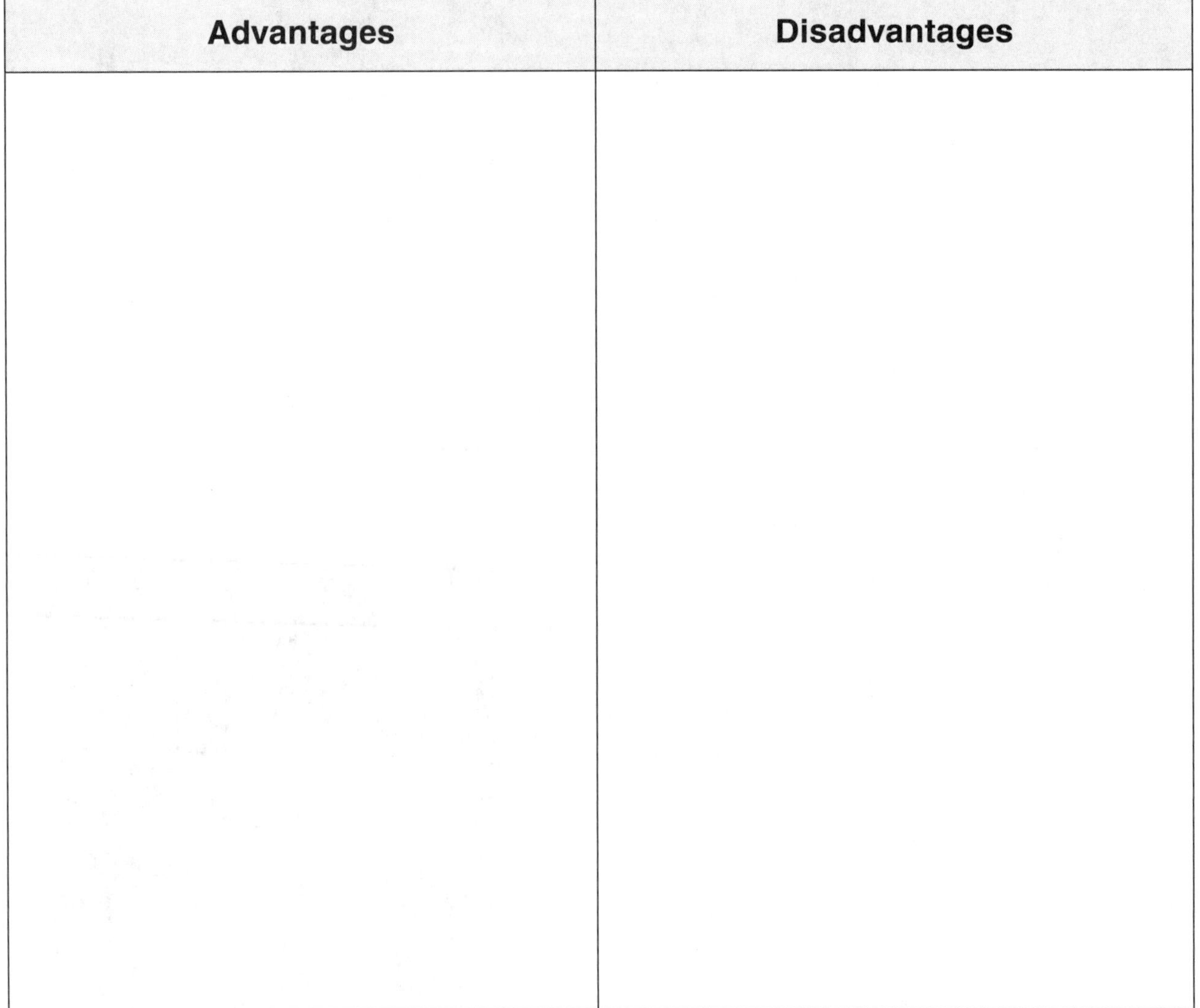

Advantages	Disadvantages

NAME: ______________________ **DATE:** ________________

Directions: Read the opinion paragraph about solar energy. Underline details that support the opinion that solar energy should be used.

Today, many people are interested in taking care of the environment, and their answer is solar energy. Unlike traditional energy sources, solar energy does not produce any pollution. It is a clean, renewable resource, which means it will last without getting used up. Solar energy does not work well during cloudy days and cannot be used at all at night. Solar panels are expensive to install, but they're getting less expensive every year, and users save a lot of money. Once the equipment has been built and installed, there is no operating cost because sunlight is free. Of course, solar energy does not convert easily to electricity. Solar energy is an environmentally-safe way to power technology in the United States and around the world.

Cursive Practice *abc*

Directions: Use cursive to write *solar energy* on the top line. Then, use cursive to write the words *free* and *clean* on the bottom lines.

____

______________________ ______________________

NAME: ____________________ **DATE:** ______________

Directions: Read each sentence. Decide which word should go in the blank, and fill in the letter for the correct answer.

1. The solar panels are going _____, on the roof.
   - Ⓐ they're
   - Ⓑ their
   - Ⓒ there

2. _____ going to save the company a lot of money!
   - Ⓐ They're
   - Ⓑ Their
   - Ⓒ There

3. _____ are a lot of advantages to using solar energy.
   - Ⓐ They're
   - Ⓑ Their
   - Ⓒ There

4. Using _____ energy will help the environment.
   - Ⓐ they're
   - Ⓑ their
   - Ⓒ there

Boost Your Learning!

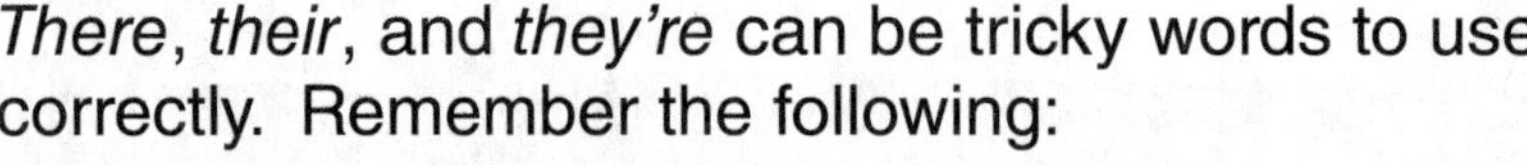

There, *their*, and *they're* can be tricky words to use correctly. Remember the following:

there: a location or place

Example: Please put your lunch over *there*.

their: belonging to people or things

Example: Buying that car is *their* choice.

they're: the contraction for *they are*

Example: *They're* moving to Florida.

NAME: ______________________ **DATE:** ________________

Directions: Read each sentence and make necessary changes. Use the ≡ symbol to show that a letter should be capitalized and the / symbol to show a letter should be lowercase. Then, fill in the table with three common and proper nouns of your choice.

1. Solar Energy is hard for cloudy, rainy countries like england.
2. Heat and energy are two products of the Sun.
3. Solar is the latin word for sun.
4. In the 1830s, a man named john herschel used solar energy to cook Food.
5. The energy can be stored in Batteries to use during the Night.

Common Nouns	Proper Nouns

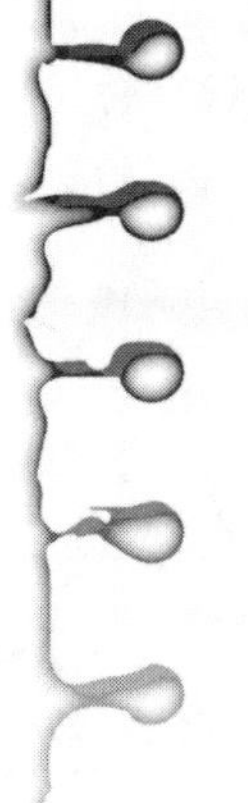

Boost Your Learning!

- A **common noun** names a **general** person, place, or thing. It is always lowercase.

  Examples: *girl*, *country*, and *monument*
- A **proper noun** names a **specific** person, place, or thing. It is always capitalized.

  Examples: *Sarah*, *India*, **and** *Lincoln Memorial*

NAME: ______________________ **DATE:** ______________

Directions: Read the opinion paragraph. Then, answer the question.

Today, many people are interested in taking care of the environment, and their answer is solar energy. Unlike traditional energy sources, solar energy does not produce any pollution. It is a clean, renewable resource, which means it will last without getting used up. Solar energy does not work well during cloudy days and cannot be used at all at night. Solar panels are expensive to install, but they're getting less expensive every year, and users save a lot of money. Once the equipment has been built and installed, there is no operating cost because sunlight is free. Solar energy is an environmentally-safe way to power technology in the United States and around the world.

This week I learned: 

- to support my opinion with information
- to use *there*, *their*, and *they're* correctly
- to capitalize proper nouns

1. What advice would you give to the author for how to improve the paragraph?

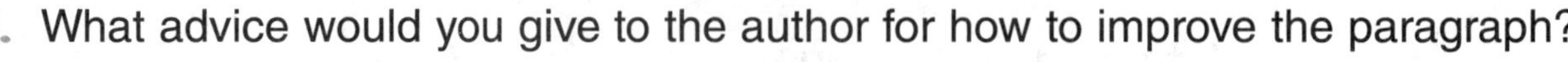

____

NAME: ______________________ **DATE:** ______________

Directions: Turbines are a way of harnessing and using wind as energy. Read the notes about using turbines. Decide if each note is an advantage or a disadvantage, and write it in the table below.

- no wind, no energy
- tall, but do not take up much land
- noisy to nearby homes and businesses
- birds killed by turbine blades
- wind is free
- does not create pollution or greenhouse gases
- clutter land, which some people say is ugly
- good for remote areas without access to electricity

Advantages	Disadvantages

NAME: ______________________ **DATE:** ________________

Directions: Do you think turbines should be used to collect wind energy? Write your opinion and why you feel the way you do. Use the table from page 139 to help you draft your opinion paragraph.

Remember!

A strong opinion paragraph includes:

- an introductory sentence that states your opinion
- details to support your ideas
- a concluding sentence

Cursive Practice

Directions: Use cursive to write a sentence about an interesting turbine fact.

NAME: ______________________ **DATE:** ______________

Directions: Write one sentence for each of the homophones *there*, *their*, and *they're*. The sentences must be about turbines or wind energy. Use the notes on page 139 to help you.

1. ____

____

____

2. ____

____

____

3. ____

____

____

Time to Improve! 

Revisit the paragraph you wrote on page 140 about turbines. Carefully check that you used *there*, *their*, and *they're* correctly.

Remember! 

- *There* is a location or place.
- *Their* shows belonging to people or things.
- *They're* is the contraction for *they are*.

NAME: ______________________ **DATE:** ______________

Directions: Read the paragraph. Use the ≡ or / symbols to correct the capitalization errors.

Though giant Turbines are relatively new, Windmills have been around for over 1,000 years. The first windmill was built in the First Century by persians in the middle east. The idea spread to europeans in the 1200s. Windmills were used mainly to pump Water and grind Grain. Over the next few hundred years, the english and dutch made a lot of improvements to their designs. In the mid-1800s, people in the united states of america began using Windmills. Turbines, the modern windmills, are now increasingly popular ways to create Energy.

Remember! 

- Common nouns are lowercase.
- Proper nouns are capitalized.

Time to Improve! 

Do you have all of the common nouns lowercase and the proper nouns capitalized correctly in the paragraph you wrote on page 140? Double check to make sure!

NAME: ____________________ **DATE:** ____________________

Directions: Do you think turbines should be used to collect wind energy? Write your opinion and why you feel the way you do.

Prewriting
Mount Everest

NAME: ______________________ **DATE:** ________________

Directions: Mount Everest, located in the Himalayas between Nepal and Tibet, is the world's tallest mountain. The table has information that supports two opinions on whether people younger than 18 should be allowed to climb Mount Everest. Put exclamation points by sentences you think create strong arguments.

Yes
_____ Being allowed to climb should be based on capability not age. _____ If a child's parent allows it, the officials at Mount Everest should not interfere. _____ Reaching the top, or summit, would be very exciting for a teen. _____ Climbing promotes a healthy lifestyle, which could positively influence peers.
No
_____ It's dangerous because hundreds of people have died trying to reach the top. _____ Teens' brains are not fully developed to make big decisions. _____ Altitude sickness may affect young people differently from adults. _____ Mountain climbing is too expensive for teens to participate in.

NAME: ______________________ **DATE:** ______________

Directions: Read the opinion paragraph about allowing people younger than 18 to climb Mount Everest. Underline sentences that strongly support the opinion.

Climbing Mount Everest is a big accomplishment for anyone, and those younger than 18 should have a chance to climb it. Being physically fit and well-trained are important for climbing, but these things are not related to age. Many teens are in better shape than people in their 30s. Teens who climb are promoting healthy lifestyles, which could be positive influences on their peers. Reaching the summit would be very exciting for a young person. It is also very expensive. Parents know their children best, and if they give their permission, the Mount Everest officials should not interfere. People of all ages should be allowed the thrill of experiencing the summit.

Remember! 

A strong opinion paragraph includes:

- an introductory sentence stating your opinion
- details that support your opinion
- a concluding sentence restating your opinion

Cursive Practice *abc*

Directions: Use cursive to write *Mount Everest* on the top line. Then, write two adjectives to describe the mountain on the bottom lines.

____

______________________ ______________________

Revising

Mount Everest

NAME: ____________________ **DATE:** ____________

Directions: Read each sentence. Choose the antonym for each bold word.

1. Many climbers **hire** Sherpas as guides.
   Ⓐ rent
   Ⓑ dismiss
   Ⓒ need

2. A Sherpa guide can **earn** more than $5,000 during the two-month climbing season.
   Ⓐ lose
   Ⓑ make
   Ⓒ save

3. Most people in Nepal make about $50 a month, so guides are very **wealthy**.
   Ⓐ extravagant
   Ⓑ poor
   Ⓒ intelligent

4. The guides have a very **dangerous** occupation.
   Ⓐ exciting
   Ⓑ risky
   Ⓒ harmless

5. Many Sherpa guides have climbed Mount Everest **numerous** times.
   Ⓐ multiple
   Ⓑ several
   Ⓒ limited

6. Climbing Mount Everest is a **big** accomplishment.
   Ⓐ small
   Ⓑ fast
   Ⓒ exciting

Boost Your Learning! 

Antonyms are words that have the opposite meanings.

Examples: *near* and *far*, *heavy* and *light*, and *good* and *bad*

NAME: ____________________________ **DATE:** ___________________

Directions: Complete each sentence with the correct usage of *who* or *whom*.

1. With __________ are you climbing?
2. The Sherpa, __________ is an expert, will be our guide.
3. People __________ have asthma should be cautious on a climb.
4. He doesn't know to __________ he should give the tent.
5. We want to know __________ will reach the top first.

Boost Your Learning!

To figure out if you should use *who* or *whom*, try this easy tip!

Who: Replace *who* with *he* or *they*. If that part of the sentence still makes sense, *who* is the right word.

Examples

- I wonder **who** is going to the mall (. . . **he** is going to the mall).
- She met the other girls **who** are kind (. . . **they** are kind).

Whom: Replace *whom* with *him* or *them*. If that part of the sentence still makes sense, *whom* is the right word.

Examples

- **To whom** is the letter addressed? (The letter is addressed to **him**).
- He saw three men, one of **whom** is a baseball player (. . . one of **them** is a baseball player).

NAME: ______________________ **DATE:** ________________

Directions: Revisit the opinion paragraph about Mount Everest. Think about what you have learned this week. Write notes in the margins explaining how the author could improve the paragraph.

Climbing Mount Everest is a big accomplishment for anyone, and those younger than 18 should have a chance to climb it. Being physically fit and well-trained are important for climbing, but they are not related to age. Many teens are in better shape than people in their 30s. Teens who climb are promoting healthy lifestyles, which could be positive influences on their peers. Reaching the summit would be very exciting for a young person. It is also very expensive. Parents know their children, and if they give their permission, the Mount Everest officials should not be able to stop young people from attempting the climb. People of all ages should be allowed the thrill of the summit.

This week I learned: 

- to use supporting details
- about antonyms
- to use *who* and *whom* correctly

NAME: ____________________________ **DATE:** ___________________

Directions: Read the information about Mount Kilimanjaro. Then, use the information to write your thoughts about whether or not you would want to climb Mount Kilimanjaro.

Mount Kilimanjaro is in Tanzania, a country along the eastern coast of Africa. At approximately 19,340 feet (5,895 meters), it is the tallest peak in Africa. It takes six to nine days to climb to the top. About 25,000 people attempt the climb each year. Over 16,000 of them are successful. Those who do not make it to the top generally turn back because of altitude sickness. There are about 10 to 15 deaths a year on Mount Kilimanjaro.

Would you want to climb Mount Kilimanjaro?

Reasons for Climbing	Reasons for Not Climbing

Drafting
Mount Kilimanjaro

NAME: ______________________ **DATE:** ______________

Directions: Would you climb Mount Kilimanjaro? Explain the reasons for why you would or would not climb Mount Kilimanjaro. Use the table from page 149 to help you draft your opinion paragraph.

Remember!

A strong opinion paragraph includes:

- an introductory sentence
- details that support your opinion
- a concluding sentence

Cursive Practice

Directions: Use cursive to write *Tanzania*, *Africa*, and *Mount Kilimanjaro*.

NAME: ______________________ **DATE:** ________________

Directions: The sentences below are incorrect. Write an antonym for the underlined word to make each sentence true.

1. Mount Kilimanjaro is the shortest free-standing mountain, which means it is not part of a mountain range.

   ____

2. January through March are the coldest months in Tanzania.

   ____

3. The mountain's national park closed in 1977.

   ____

4. The youngest person to reach the summit was an 87-year-old Frenchman.

   ____

5. The last recorded summit of Mount Kilimanjaro was in 1889.

   ____

Remember! 

Antonyms are words that have opposite definitions.

NAME: ____________________ **DATE:** ______________

Directions: Read each sentence. If it uses *who* or *whom* correctly, write a *C* on the line. If it is incorrect, write *I* and rewrite the sentence correctly.

_____ 1. With <u>whom</u> are you hiking?

____

_____ 2. <u>Whom</u> is wearing the boots?

____

_____ 3. <u>Who</u> is going to be our guide?

____

_____ 4. To <u>who</u> will you give the pack?

____

_____ 5. <u>Who</u> will take our picture?

____

Time to Improve! 

Look over the paragraph you wrote on page 150 about Mount Kilimanjaro for *who* and *whom*. Use the replacement tips to make sure you used these words correctly!

Remember! 

- Replace *who* with *he* or *they* to see if it makes sense.
- Replace *whom* with *him* or *them* to see if it makes sense.

NAME: ______________________ **DATE:** ______________

Directions: Would you climb Mount Kilimanjaro? Explain the reasons for why you would or would not climb Mount Kilimanjaro.

NAME: ____________________ **DATE:** ______________

Directions: Read the notes. They contain information for a paragraph about creating ice sculptures. Place check marks in the circles that strongly support the main topic.

Creating Ice Sculptures

- Swan sculptures are popular for weddings.
- No cloudy or cracked ice is used.
- It can be made with a mold.
- It can be made by hand using chainsaws, drills, and chisels.
- Clear ice is made by shooting air into the water as it freezes.
- Competitions and displays are all over the world.
- The temperatures of events determine how long sculptures last.
- It can be made by a rotating machine called a *lathe.*
- It is heated by a blowtorch at the end to make them shiny.

NAME: ______________________ **DATE:** ________________

Directions: Read the informative/explanatory paragraph about creating ice sculptures. Underline sentences that strongly support the main idea.

An ice sculpture is a beautiful and dramatic way to decorate for a special event. For example, swans are very popular at weddings. Ice for a sculpture must be completely clear. To make perfect ice, air jets are used to blow air into the water as it freezes. Sculptures can be made by hand, but artists typically use chainsaws and chisels to create them. Machines called *lathes* can create sculptures quickly and efficiently. Molds can also be used. A small blowtorch is used to make the sculpture shiny after the carving is complete. The colder it is, the longer a sculpture will last. Ice sculptures are imaginative forms of art.

Cursive Practice *abc*

Directions: Use cursive to write the names of four places you think would be safe for an ice sculpture to be outside.

______________________ ______________________

______________________ ______________________

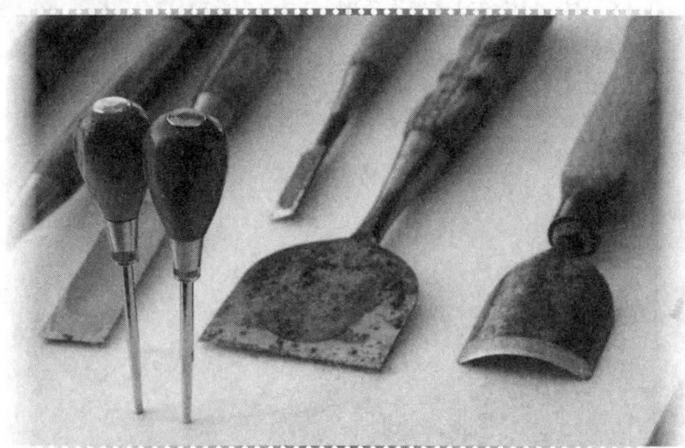

NAME: ______________________________ **DATE:** ____________________

Directions: Underline the prepositional phrases in each sentence.

1. An ice sculpture is a beautiful and dramatic way to decorate for a special event.

2. To make perfect ice, air jets are used to blow air into the water as it freezes.

3. Sculptures can be made by hand, but artists typically use chainsaws and chisels to create them.

4. A small blowtorch is used to make the sculpture shiny after the carving is complete.

5. Write a sentence with at least one prepositional phrase about ice sculpting.

____

____

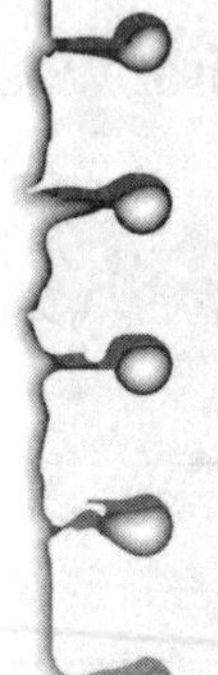

Boost Your Learning!

A **prepositional phrase** begins with a preposition such as *for*, *to*, *after*, *in*, and *over*, and can end with a noun, a verb, or an adjective.

Examples

- I shove the box under my bed.
- I gave up after trying for an hour.

NAME: ______________________ **DATE:** ________________

Directions: Read each sentence. Decide which word should go in the blank and fill in the letter for the correct answer.

1. People are not _____ to touch ice sculptures.

   Ⓐ allowed

   Ⓑ aloud

2. The sculpture will last _____ the evening.

   Ⓐ threw

   Ⓑ through

3. The artist does not know _____ or not he will finish on time.

   Ⓐ weather

   Ⓑ whether

4. The _____ made the ice shine under the light.

   Ⓐ mist

   Ⓑ missed

5. I enjoyed all of the sculptures _____ one.

   Ⓐ except

   Ⓑ accept

6. The sculptor changed the ice from _____ to smooth.

   Ⓐ course

   Ⓑ coarse

Remember! 

Homophones are words that sound the same but have different meanings. They may or may not be spelled the same.

Examples: *knows* and *nose*, *hear* and *here*

NAME: ______________________ **DATE:** ______________

Publishing
Sculpture

Directions: Read the paragraph. Then, answer the question.

An ice sculpture is a beautiful and dramatic way to decorate for a special event. For example, swans are very popular at weddings. Ice for a sculpture must be completely clear. To make perfect ice, air jets are used to blow air into the water as it freezes. Sculptures can be made by hand, and artists typically use chainsaws and chisels to create them. Machines called *lathes* can create sculptures quickly and efficiently. Molds can also be used. A small blowtorch is used to make the sculpture shiny after the carving is complete. The colder it is, the longer a sculpture will last. Ice sculptures are imaginative forms of art.

This week I learned: 

- to support the main idea with strong details
- about prepositional phrases
- to use homophones correctly

1. How could the paragraph be stronger? Give at least two suggestions.

____

____

____

____

NAME: ______________________ **DATE:** ________________

Directions: Look at the web for information about a style of painting called *abstract*. Place check marks in the circles that strongly support the main topic.

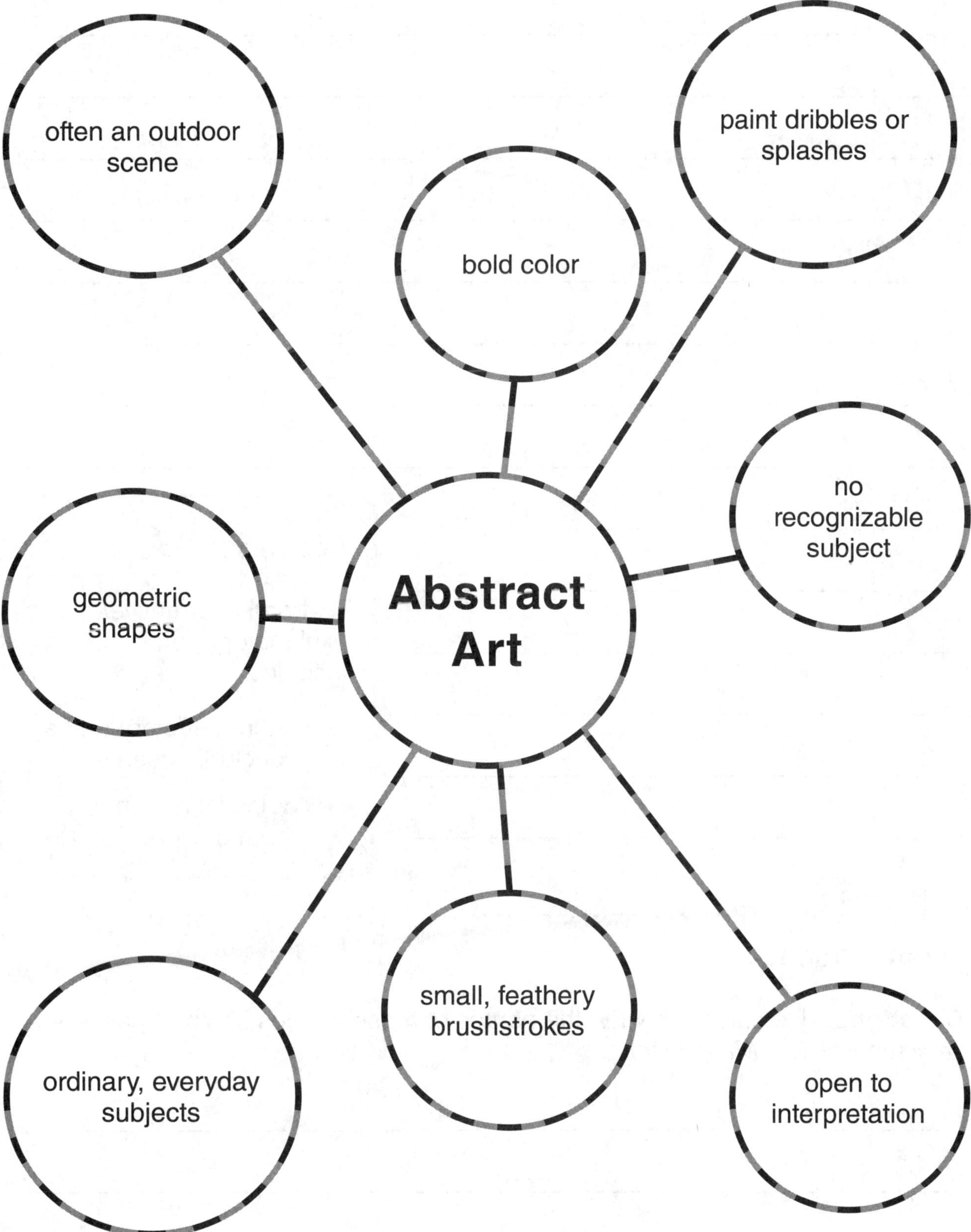

Drafting
Painting

NAME: ______________________ **DATE:** ______________

Directions: Describe what abstract art is. Include facts about what abstract art looks like. Use the web on page 159 and your own observations to help you draft your informative/explanatory paragraph.

Remember!

A strong informative/explanatory paragraph includes:

- an introductory and a concluding sentence
- details that support the main idea

Cursive Practice

Directions: Use cursive to write the names of these famous abstract painters: *Jackson Pollock*, *Mark Rothko*.

NAME: ____________________ **DATE:** ____________________

Directions: Improve each sentence by adding a prepositional phrase. Use the prepositions in parentheses to help you.

1. Anyone can learn to paint. (*by*)

   ____

   ____

2. Budding artists can take lessons. (*from*)

   ____

   ____

3. They can observe nature. (*around*)

   ____

   ____

4. Painting may not be easy. (*until*)

   ____

   ____

Time to Improve! 

Sometimes a prepositional phrase can add a detail or make a sentence more interesting. Reread the paragraph you wrote on page 160 and see if any sentences can be improved by adding prepositional phrases.

NAME: ______________________ **DATE:** ________________

Directions: Read the sentences. They all have incorrect homophones. Use the ℘ and ∧ symbols to correct them.

1. No one nose what the painting is supposed to be about.
2. The hole painting is filled with different colors.
3. The group had to weight in line at the art museum.
4. The bear canvas came alive with the interesting painting.
5. A flour is not an abstract subject.
6. The dark colors in the painting feel like knight.
7. It looks like a pale of paint was splashed on the artwork.
8. Many people want to meat the artist.

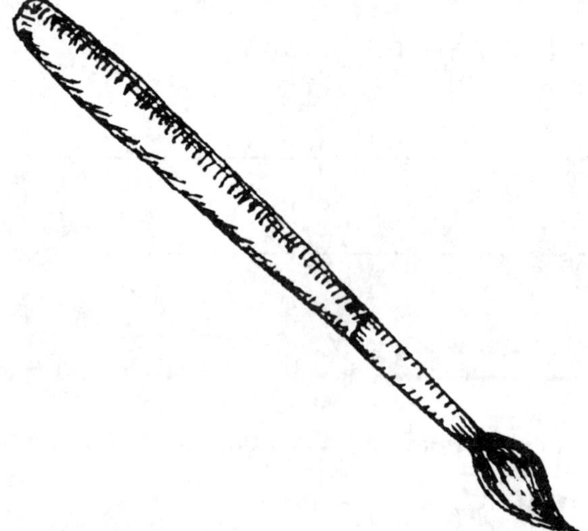

Time to Improve! 

Revisit the paragraph you wrote on page 160 for homophones. If you find any, make sure they are correct.

NAME: ____________________ **DATE:** ____________________

Directions: Describe what abstract art is. Include facts about what abstract art looks like.

NAME: ______________________ **DATE:** ______________

Directions: Look at the table about steam engine trains. The first column has facts. The second column is supposed to show that the facts are advantages for steam engine trains. If it is an advantage, put a star by the sentence. If it is not an advantage, put an *X*.

Facts	Advantages
Steam engines do not need to be by water sources.	_____ The engines can be anywhere instead of being stuck by a river or a lake.
Steam engines produce lots of smoke.	_____ The smoke puts air pollution into the environment.
Steam engines are powerful.	_____ One steam engine is equal to the power of many horses.
The steam in a steam engine's boiler room is under tremendous pressure.	_____ Boilers can burst, leading to loss of workers' lives and property.
Steam engines can be used at any time.	_____ Other energy sources, like wind, can only be used under the right weather conditions.

NAME: ______________________ **DATE:** ______________

Directions: Read the opinion paragraph about the advantages of a steam engine train. Underline sentences that support the main idea.

Though steam engine trains were not perfect, they were the right choice for transportation at the time and made travel easier. Most power before the 1800s required being close to water sources, but the steam engine train allowed distance from water. Windmills provided another kind of power but depended on the wind and weather; steam engine trains could work regardless of the environment. Trains burned wood to heat water and create steam, and the smoke produced by the burning wood added to air pollution. The steam was under tremendous pressure and sometimes caused boilers to burst, injuring people and destroying property. Horses were commonly used for travel, but a steam engine train was equal to the power of many horses. Steam engine trains eventually gave way to gasoline engines, but they were very important during their time.

Cursive Practice *abc*

Directions: Use cursive to write one question you have about steam engine trains.

____

____

Revising

Steam Engine Trains

NAME: ______________________ **DATE:** ________________

Directions: Read each sentence. The answer choices are words that have similar but not identical meanings. Fill in the bubble with the best answer for each sentence.

1. Though the steam engine train had existed for a long time, people were _____ for ways to improve it.
   Ⓐ exploring
   Ⓑ searching

2. It will take several months to build a railroad bridge over the _____.
   Ⓐ pond
   Ⓑ lake

3. It is _____ for one horse to do the work a steam engine train can.
   Ⓐ impossible
   Ⓑ difficult

4. The steam engine train easily makes its way over the gentle _____ of the land.
   Ⓐ hills
   Ⓑ mountains

Boost Your Learning!

Synonyms are words that have similar meanings. Oftentimes, a synonym has a different feel or intensity from another.

Examples

- I skipped breakfast and was <u>hungry</u> by lunch.
- During the famine, many children were <u>starving</u>.

NAME: ____________________ **DATE:** ____________

Directions: Look at the underlined possessive noun in each sentence. If it is correct, put a *C* on the line. If it is incorrect, put an *I* on the line and rewrite the possessive noun correctly.

_____ 1. America's first steam engine railway opened in 1830.

____

_____ 2. Coal and water were stored in a trains tender, which is a wagon pulled behind the train.

____

_____ 3. Many railway station's arrival and departure times were different because there was not a national standard time until 1883.

____

_____ 4. It took three hours of workers' time to get a steam engine train moving.

____

Boost Your Learning!

- A **possessive noun** means something belongs to the noun. You show this by adding an apostrophe and an *-s* to the end of the noun.

  Example: a girl's backpack (the backpack belongs to one girl)

- A **plural possessive noun** means something belongs to a plural noun. You show this by adding an apostrophe to the end of the noun.

  Example: the boys' classroom (the classroom belongs to more than one boy)

NAME: ______________________ **DATE:** ________________

Directions: Reread the paragraph about steam engine trains. Think about what you practiced this week. In the margins, write at least three ways to improve the paragraph.

Though steam engine trains were not perfect, they were the right choice for transportation at the time and made travel easier. Most power before the 1800s required being close to water sources, but the steam engine train allowed distance from water. Windmills provided another kind of power but depended on the wind and weather; steam engine trains could work regardless of the environment. Trains burned wood to heat water and create steam, and the smoke produced by the burning wood added to air pollution. The steam was under tremendous pressure and sometimes caused boilers to burst, injuring people and destroying property. Horses were commonly used for travel, but a steam engine train was equal to the power of many horses. Steam engine trains eventually gave way to gasoline engines, but they were very important during their time.

This week I learned: 

- to include strong supporting details
- to use precise words
- about possessive nouns

NAME: ______________________ **DATE:** ________________

Directions: Complete the chart by putting a check mark for each fact in the appropriate column based on whether or not bullet trains are a good idea. Then, write why you think the fact is an advantage or a disadvantage.

Fact	Advantage	Disadvantage	Why?
There are over 15 countries with bullet trains.			
Americans tend to prefer the freedom of driving their own cars.			
California has plans to build a bullet train with an estimated cost of $98.5 billion.			
Bullet trains travel a minimum of 155 mph (249 kph).			
Bullet trains use electricity.			

NAME: ______________________ DATE: ________________

Directions: Should the United States construct its own bullet trains? Explain your opinion and why you feel the way you do. Use the table on page 169 to help you draft your opinion paragraph.

Remember!

A strong opinion paragraph includes:

- an introductory sentence stating your opinion
- strong supporting details
- a concluding sentence

Cursive Practice

Directions: Write the names of these countries that have bullet trains in cursive: *Spain*, *Japan*, *Russia*, and *France*.

NAME: ______________________ **DATE:** ______________

Directions: Read each pair of sentences. They are the same except for the underlined words, which have similar, but not identical, meanings. On the lines, explain the differences between the words.

1. The passenger was <u>wandering</u> toward the train station.

   The passenger was <u>walking</u> toward the train station.

   ____

   ____

2. As she boarded the train, she <u>glared</u> at the man behind her.

   As she boarded the train, she <u>stared</u> at the man behind her.

   ____

   ____

3. <u>Tossing</u> her bag on the floor, she took a seat.

   <u>Hurling</u> her bag on the floor, she took a seat.

   ____

   ____

4. She remembered the <u>argument</u> between two of the passengers.

   She remembered the <u>disagreement</u> between two of the passengers.

   ____

   ____

Time to Improve! 

Reread the paragraph you wrote on page 170. Make sure the words you use express the meanings you want. If they don't, use synonyms.

NAME: ____________________ **DATE:** ____________

Directions: Write the possessive form of the nouns in parentheses for each sentence.

1. ________________ (Japan) bullet train is called *Shinkansen* which means "new trunk lines."

2. The ________________ (bullet train) debut was October 1, 1964, but it has had many updates since its beginning.

3. ________________ (Passengers) safety is a priority, and there has never been a fatal accident.

4. The train ________________ (system) average delay is only 36 seconds.

5. Other ________________ (countries) designs have used the *Shinkansen* as an inspiration.

Time to Improve! 

Do you have any possessive nouns in your paragraph? If so, make sure you used an apostrophe correctly.

Remember! 

A quick tip for possessive nouns:

- engineer's schedule (schedule belonging to the engineer)
- families' items (items belonging to more than one family)

NAME: ______________________ **DATE:** ______________

Directions: Should the United States construct its own bullet trains? Explain your opinion and why you feel the way you do.

Prewriting
Eiffel Tower

NAME: ______________________________ **DATE:** ____________________

Directions: Read the narrative notes in the flowchart. Put stars by six to eight things you think should be in a narrative paragraph about a girl visiting the Eiffel Tower in Paris, France.

BEGINNING

_____ last day in Paris

_____ went to a museum the day before

_____ finally at the Eiffel Tower

MIDDLE

_____ insisted on walking up the 1,665 stairs of the tower

_____ not crowded on stairs

_____ very busy at the top

_____ could see for miles

END

_____ there at dusk when lights turned on

_____ took elevator down

_____ favorite memory of Paris

NAME: ______________________ **DATE:** ________________

Directions: Read the narrative paragraph about Aaliyah visiting the Eiffel Tower. Underline sentences you think should stay in the story.

Aaliyah felt like butterflies were fluttering in her stomach. It was her last day in Paris, and she was finally going to see the Eiffel Tower. Yesterday, her tour group had visited a museum. Most of the others wanted to take the elevator, but Aaliyah insisted on going up the old-fashioned way. She climbed up all 1,665 steps to get to the top. The stairs were not busy, but the top of the tower was like a zoo. As she looked over Paris, she saw clouds like cotton balls and a sunset striping the sky. She could see for miles. The sun slipped below the horizon and the lights on the Eiffel Tower turned on. They were as bright as the sun. Tired but happy, Aaliyah took the elevator down with the rest of her group. This would definitely be her favorite memory of Paris.

Remember! 

A strong narrative paragraph should:

- have a beginning, a middle, and an end
- sound like a story
- have interesting details

Cursive Practice *abc*

Directions: Use cursive to write *Paris, France*.

____

NAME: ______________________ **DATE:** ________________

Directions: Write *S* if the sentence includes a simile. Write *M* if the sentence includes a metaphor. Then, underline the simile or metaphor in each sentence.

_____ 1. Aaliyah feels like butterflies are in her stomach.

_____ 2. The top of the tower is a zoo.

_____ 3. The sunset stripes the sky in color.

_____ 4. She sees clouds like cotton balls.

_____ 5. The lights are as bright as the sun.

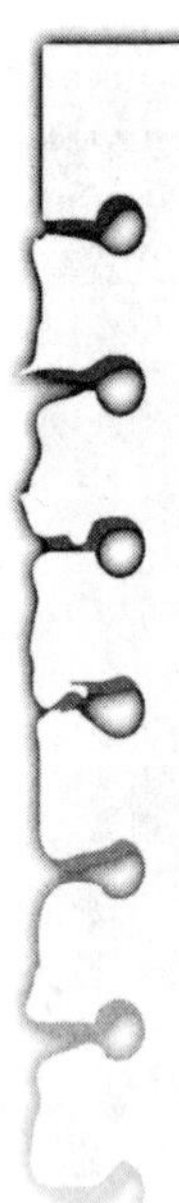

Boost Your Learning!

Using similes and metaphors can make your writing more exciting!

- A **simile** compares two unlike things using the words *like* or *as*.

  Example: John is *as strong as an ox*.

- A **metaphor** compares two things without using *like* or *as*.

  Example: Jenna's hair *is red fire*.

NAME: ____________________ **DATE:** ____________________

Directions: Read each sentence and look for capitalization errors. Use the ≡ and / symbols to correct the errors.

1. the eiffel tower was built in 1889.
2. It was built to be the Entrance Arch for the world's fair.
3. The Tower is repainted every seven years to protect it from Rust.
4. There are 20,000 Lightbulbs on the Eiffel tower.
5. It was almost torn down but was kcpt because it could be used as a Radio Antenna.

Remember! 

Proper nouns are the names of specific people, places, and things. They should always be capitalized.

Examples

- *city* (common noun) and *New York City* (proper noun)
- *statue* (common noun) and *Statue of Liberty* (proper noun)

NAME: ______________________ **DATE:** ________________

Directions: Reread the paragraph about Aaliyah's visit to the Eiffel Tower. Think about what you have learned this week. Use the margins to write three ways the paragraph can be improved.

Aaliyah felt like butterflies were fluttering in her stomach. It was her last day in paris, and she was finally going to see the Eiffel tower. Yesterday, her Tour Group had visited a Museum. Most of the others wanted to take the elevator, but Aaliyah insisted on going up the old-fashioned way. She climbed up all 1,665 steps to get to the top. The stairs were not busy, but the top of the tower was like a zoo. As she looked over paris, she saw clouds like cotton balls and a sunset striping the sky. She could see for miles. The sun slipped below the horizon and the lights on the Eiffel tower turned on. They were as bright as the sun. Tired but happy, Aaliyah took the elevator down with the rest of her group. This would definitely be her favorite memory of paris.

This week I learned: 

- to include a beginning, a middle, and an end
- about similes and metaphors
- to capitalize proper nouns

NAME: ______________________ **DATE:** ________________

Directions: Read the paragraph about the Leaning Tower of Pisa in Italy. Use the information as well as your imagination to brainstorm ideas for a narrative paragraph about a student's visit to the Leaning Tower of Pisa. Then, write your ideas in the flowchart.

The Leaning Tower of Pisa in Pisa, Italy, is one of the most famous towers in the world because of its tilt. The circular, 8-story building leans because of the soft ground underneath. It is 183 feet (56 meters) tall on its sinking side and almost 186 feet (57 meters) tall on the other side. There are 294 or 296 steps to reach the top, depending on which side a person climbs. The tower was built as a freestanding bell tower for the cathedral in Pisa. Construction started in 1173 and took over 200 years to complete.

BEGINNING

MIDDLE

END

NAME: ______________________ **DATE:** ______________

Directions: Imagine a time when a student visits the Leaning Tower of Pisa. Include details that describe how the student felt and what he or she saw. Use your flowchart on page 179 to help you draft your narrative paragraph.

Remember!

A strong narrative paragraph should:

- have a beginning, a middle, and an end
- sound like a story
- have interesting details

Cursive Practice

Directions: Write the location of the Leaning Tower of Pisa in cursive: *Piazza del Duomo in Pisa, Italy*.

NAME: ____________________ **DATE:** ______________

Directions: Complete each sentence with a phrase from the Phrase Bank. If the sentence contains a simile, write *S* before the sentence. If it contains a metaphor, write *M*.

Phrase Bank

as an arrow | moths to a flame | light of Pisa | as a fishhook

_____ 1. The Leaning Tower of Pisa is not as straight

____________________.

_____ 2. In fact, it is as crooked ____________________.

_____ 3. The tower is the ____________________.

_____ 4. People are drawn to visit it like ____________________.

Time to Improve! 

Have you included any similes or metaphors in the narrative paragraph you wrote on page 180? If not, go back and try to add one or two to make your writing more exciting.

Remember! 

- Similes make comparisons using the words *like* or *as*.
- Metaphors make comparisons without the words *like* or *as*.

NAME: ______________________ **DATE:** ________________

Directions: Use the ≡ and / symbols to correct the sentences. Then, write why you made the changes you did.

1. during world war II, the leaning tower of pisa was almost destroyed.

____

____

2. many tall buildings in italy were being used as lookout towers by nazis.

____

____

3. american soldiers were ordered to bomb any potential lookouts.

____

____

4. the beauty of the leaning tower of pisa saved it from destruction.

____

____

Time to Improve! 

Reread the paragraph you wrote on page 180 and pay careful attention to nouns. Make sure all proper nouns are capitalized correctly.

NAME: ______________________ **DATE:** ________________

Directions: Imagine a time when a student visits the Leaning Tower of Pisa. Include details that describe how the student feels and what he or she sees.

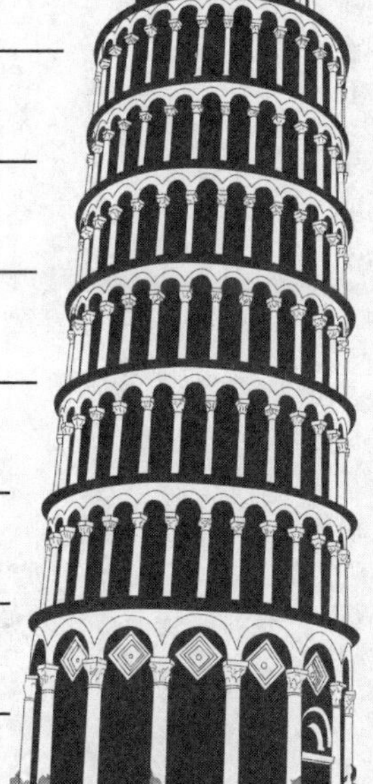

NAME: ______________________________ **DATE:** ____________________

Directions: Read the notes about a camping trip. Put stars by five to seven items you think would be interesting to include in a personal narrative about camping.

_____ I was excited to go on my first camping trip.

_____ Everything seemed to go wrong.

_____ We couldn't get the tent set up.

_____ My mom forgot the cooler with the drinks.

_____ I wanted to go hiking.

_____ Dad worked for over an hour to start the fire.

_____ My little sister was scared of bears.

_____ I dropped my hot dog into the fire.

_____ When we finally got settled, it started to rain.

NAME: ______________________ **DATE:** ______________

Directions: Read the personal narrative. Underline sentences you think belong in the paragraph.

I had been looking forward to my first camping trip for weeks. I was very excited when we finally left Friday after school. Things started off smoothly, but it didn't take long before everything seemed to go wrong. We pulled our brand new tent out of its bag and began setting it up. We realized a pole was missing, so it was impossible to put together. My dad said we could sleep under the beautiful sky. We were hungry for dinner. My dad started building a fire, but it took him over an hour to get it going. I was not waiting patiently. My mom went to get the cooler with drinks out of the truck but came back empty-handed. She forgot the cooler at home. As darkness began to fall, I was hungry, thirsty, and cranky. I laid out my sleeping bag, feeling hopeful I could see the stars. It's too cloudy I said to myself, and that's when the first raindrop splashed on my cheek.

Cursive Practice *abc*

Directions: Use cursive to write four things you would need to bring on a camping trip.

______________________ ______________________

______________________ ______________________

NAME: ______________________ **DATE:** ________________

Directions: Use the suffixes in the Suffix Bank to complete the words in each sentence. You may use a suffix more than once.

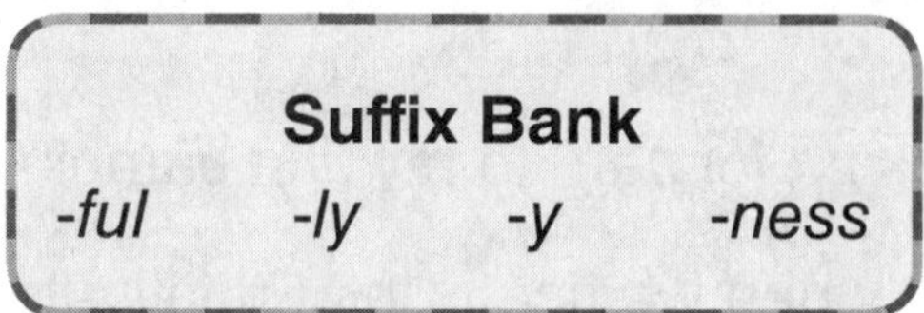

Suffix Bank			
-ful	*-ly*	*-y*	*-ness*

1. Things start off smooth_____.
2. I cannot wait patient_____.
3. Dark_____ begins to fall.
4. I feel hope_____ about seeing stars.
5. It is a cloud_____ night.

Boost Your Learning!

A **suffix** is a letter or group of letters added to the end of a word that slightly changes the word's meaning.

Examples
dark → dark**er**
friend → friend**ly**

NAME: ______________________ **DATE:** ________________

Directions: Use the ∨ symbol to insert commas and quotation marks in the dialogue. Then, write a line of dialogue to respond.

1. My dad said we can sleep under the beautiful sky.

____

____

2. I forgot the cooler at home she said.

____

____

3. It's too cloudy my sister said to herself.

____

____

Remember! 

Tips for using quotation marks:

- Put quotation marks around anything people say out loud.
- The quotation should start with a capital letter.
- Use a comma to separate what was said from who said it.

  Example: "Camping is a fun way to experience nature," said the tour guide.

NAME: ____________________ **DATE:** ________________

Publishing
Camping

Directions: Read the paragraph. Think about what you have learned this week. Write in the margins to explain three ways the author could improve the paragraph.

I had been looking forward to my first camping trip for weeks. I was very excited when we finally left Friday after school. Things started off smoothly, but it didn't take long before everything seemed to go wrong. We pulled our brand new tent out of its bag and began setting it up. We realized a pole was missing, so it was impossible to put together. My dad said we could sleep under the beautiful sky. We were hungry for dinner. My dad started building a fire, but it took him over an hour to get it going. I was not waiting patiently. My mom went to get the cooler with drinks out of the truck but came back empty-handed. She forgot the cooler at home. As darkness began to fall, I was hungry, thirsty, and cranky. I laid out my sleeping bag, feeling hopeful I could see the stars. It's too cloudy I said to myself, and that's when the first raindrop splashed on my cheek.

This week I learned: 

- to include interesting information in narratives
- about different suffixes
- to use quotation marks correctly

NAME: ______________________________ **DATE:** ____________________

Directions: Write notes that you would include in a personal narrative about a time you went swimming. Use a real experience or your imagination. Be sure to make your notes exciting and interesting.

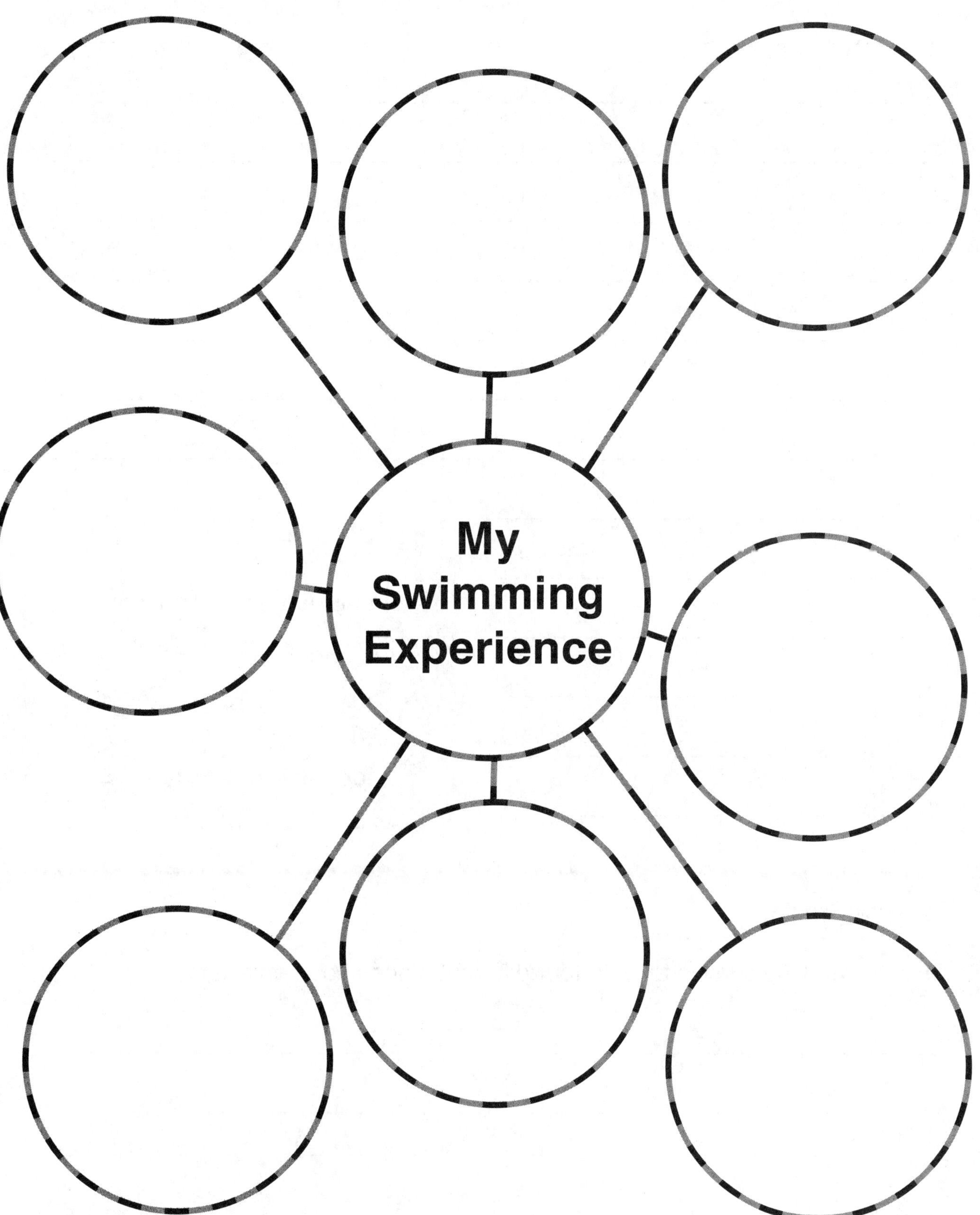

NAME: ______________________ **DATE:** ______________

Directions: Imagine a time you went swimming. Describe the experience, including where you swam and whom you swam with. Use your thoughts and ideas from page 189 to help you draft your personal narrative paragraph.

Remember!

A strong personal narrative:

- is about you
- has a beginning, a middle, and an end
- sounds like a story

Cursive Practice

Directions: Use cursive to write four different places you can swim.

NAME: ______________________ **DATE:** ______________

Directions: Read each sentence. Fill in the bubbles with the suffixes that mean the same things as the underlined phrases.

1. Being on a swim team is an activity that is <u>able to be enjoyed</u>.
   - Ⓐ enjoyable
   - Ⓑ enjoyless

2. The feeling of being <u>without weight</u> in the water is relaxing.
   - Ⓐ weightless
   - Ⓑ weightful

3. People must always be <u>full of care</u> when they are around water.
   - Ⓐ careless
   - Ⓑ careful

4. Many swimmers are <u>full of thanks</u> for their memories of being on a team.
   - Ⓐ thankful
   - Ⓑ thankless

Boost Your Learning! 

Suffixes have different meanings.

Examples

- *-able* means "able to be" (agree**able**)
- *-less* means "without" (meaning**less**)
- *-ful* means "full of" (wonder**ful**)

Time to Improve! 

Reread the personal narrative you wrote on page 190 about swimming. Make sure any suffixes you used are correct.

NAME: ______________________ **DATE:** ______________

Editing
Swimming

Directions: Read the conversation between a mother and son at the beach. Use the ∨ symbol to add quotation marks and punctuation marks to each sentence.

1. Can I go swim in the ocean the boy asked his mother.

2. Not until I am ready to go with you his mother responded.

3. The boy stomped his foot and cried I want to go now

4. It is not safe to go swimming alone his mother gently explained.

5. I understand. Are you ready now he asked with a grin.

Time to Improve! 

Have you used any dialogue in the personal narrative you wrote on page 190? If so, make sure it is used correctly. If not, consider adding some!

NAME: ______________________ **DATE:** ________________

Directions: Imagine a time you went swimming. Describe the experience, including where you swam and whom you swam with.

ANSWER KEY

The activity pages that do not have specific answers to them are not included in this answer key. Students' answers will vary on these activity pages, so check that students are staying on task.

Week 1: Hieroglyphics

Day 1 (page 14)

Hieroglyphics use symbols and pictures; Symbols point to the beginning of a line to let the reader know where to start reading; The writing contains no punctuation; There are more than 700 symbols; The Rosetta Stone helped people learn how to read the symbols; Egyptians wrote hieroglyphics on paper called *papyrus*.

Day 2 (page 15)

Underline: Over 700 symbols!; Contains no punctuation; With Greek and Egyptian written side by side.

Day 3 (page 16)

Example answers include:

1. The hieroglyphics are beautiful to look at.
2. Egyptians wrote on an early paper called *papyrus*.
3. Hieroglyphics are hard to understand.
4. The Rosetta Stone was important to translating hieroglyphics.

Day 4 (page 17)

1. Egypt is in northeastern **Africa**.
2. Makeup protected the people's **faces** from the sun.
3. The **Nile** River was important to Egypian crops.
4. Ancient Egyptians used **toothpaste**.
5. The Rosetta Stone was found by **French** soldiers.
6. The Egyptian **leader** was called a pharaoh.

Week 2: Pyramids

Day 1 (page 19)

The structures were intended to protect the pharaohs' bodies forever; Pyramids were filled with items and treasures needed for the afterlife; The pharaohs were buried in the pyramids; Family members and servants were sometimes buried in the pyramids.

Day 3 (page 21)

1. RO; The pyramids were built on the west side of the Nile River. It is known as the land of the dead.
2. F; The pyramids were built of limestone by thousands of workers.
3. RO; The Sphinx had the head of a pharaoh and the body of a lion.

Day 4 (page 22)

Capitalize: King Tut, Egypt, English, Howard

Lowercase: pharaoh, archaeologist, treasures, artifacts

Day 5 (page 23)

See Informative/Explanatory Writing Rubric on page 203.

Week 3: Hurling

Day 1 (page 24)

1. R
2. P
3. R
4. S
5. P
6. S

Day 2 (page 25)

Example answers include:

1. Passing the ball in so many different ways makes hurling more interesting than other sports.
2. Games are thrilling to watch because there is a lot of scoring.
3. Players play for pride and love of the game, which is better than professional athletes playing for money.

Day 3 (page 26)

players, nets, sports, hurlies, bails, sticks, helmets, balls, teams, hands

Day 4 (page 27)

1. Players **may** hit the ball with hurley sticks.
2. Hurlers **must** run fast to play this sport.
3. Teams **may** earn up to three points with one score.
4. A player **must** have fast reflexes in hurling.
5. The amateur players **may** receive money.

Week 4: Cricket

Day 3 (page 31)

1. Joseph will write his essays about the rules of cricket.
2. The ladies **bring** the babies to watch cricket.
3. The victories **belong** to the players.

Day 4 (page 32)

must, might, should, would

Day 5 (page 33)

See Opinion Writing Rubric on page 202.

ANSWER KEY *(cont.)*

Week 5: Cupcakes

Day 1 (page 34)

See: pink frosting, sprinkles, lit candle, large; Taste/Smell: chocolate, vanilla, sugar, sweet; Feel: moist, sticky frosting, crinkly wrapper, warm

Day 2 (page 35)

Underline: A lit, glowing candle sat in the middle of the sprinkles scattered on the icing; After making her wish and blowing out the candle, Jada peeled back the crinkly wrapper; A bit of frosting stuck to her lip as she bit into the chocolate cake; It was sweet and delicious; Breathing in the scent of vanilla, she took another bite.

Day 4 (page 37)

1. E; !
2. IN; ?
3. E; !
4. D; .
5. IM; .
6. IN; ?
7. IM; .
8. D; .

Day 5 (page 38)

1. The author could have used more sensory details in his or her writing to make it more exciting.

Week 6: Ice Cream

Day 3 (page 41)

1. Crisp and warm cones taste delicious.
2. Frozen ice cream melts on hot days.
3. Strawberries are fun, fruity choices.
4. Natural ingredients make fresh and tasty flavors.

Day 4 (page 42)

People eat ice cream cones every day**.**; But when was the cone invented**?**; Now, cones are everywhere**!**; The next time you have an ice cream cone, remember the 1904 World's Fair**.**

Day 5 (page 43)

See Narrative Rubric on page 204.

Week 7: Skeleton

Day 1 (page 44)

Babies have 300 bones, but adults have 206; The longest bone in the body is the thighbone, which is called the femur; Bones in the hands and feet make up over half of the body's bones; The smallest bone in the body is in the ear. It is smaller than a grain of rice.

Day 2 (page 45)

Example answers: The human skeleton is fascinating; The skeleton provides support to the whole body.

Day 3 (page 46)

For example; On the other hand; In fact

Day 4 (page 47)

1. definition 3
2. definition 1
3. Students answers will vary.

Day 5 (page 48)

1. The paragraph is missing good introductory and concluding sentences. It jumps right into the information.
2. Yes, the paragraph informs the reader about bones. It includes many facts about bones.

Week 8: Muscles

Day 1 (page 49)

cover skeleton and move bones; used for voluntary movement; layers of muscle control organs; used for involuntary movement; pumps the heart and blood; only in the heart

Day 3 (page 51)

1. For example
2. Since
3. On the other hand
4. but
5. In addition to

Day 5 (page 53)

See Informative/Explanatory Writing Rubric on page 203.

Week 9: Morse Code

Day 1 (page 54)

1. A
2. A
3. D
4. A
5. A
6. D
7. D

Day 2 (page 55)

Underline: Communicating through this code is fairly secure; Because not everyone knows it, it is unlikely the message will fall into the wrong hands; The equipment is inexpensive and transmitting the messages is easy; Morse Code is used all over the world and is understood by receivers in all countries.

Day 3 (page 56)

1. modern: the present time
2. transmitting: to send and receive information

Day 4 (page 57)

1. except—accept
2. loose—lose
3. Their—They're
4. capitol—capital
5. hole—whole
6. Student answers will vary.

ANSWER KEY *(cont.)*

Week 10: Telegrams

Day 3 (page 61)

1. *Agitated* means being bothered or disturbed. The context clue said Myra couldn't concentrate on her message because the room was too loud.
2. *Superfluous* means an unnecessary amount. The context clue said a one-page message was stretched to two pages.
3. *Attentive* means working carefully and paying attention. The context clue gave the definition of the word.

Day 5 (page 63)

See Opinion Writing Rubric on page 202.

Week 11: Great Danes

Day 1 (page 64)

one of the largest dog breeds; males are 120 to 200 pounds (54 to 91 kilograms), females are 100 to 130 pounds (45 to 59 kilograms); 2014 *Guinness Book of World Records'* largest dog; colors are: black, fawn (yellow gold with black "mask" on face), brindle (fawn and black swirled together), and harlequin (white with large black marks); ears can be cropped (cut so they stand up to a point) or natural (floppy)

Day 2 (page 65)

1. "The 2014 world record for largest dog was a Great Dane named Zeus." can be crossed off because it does not tell information that supports the main idea.

Day 3 (page 66)

1. RO; Great Danes have short hair**, and** it requires brushing once a week.
2. C
3. RO; Great danes need daily walks**, but** they are not high exercise dogs.
4. RO; This breed needs to be around people**, or** it could get anxious.

Day 4 (page 67)

1. will be
2. were
3. will be
4. were

Week 12: Chihuahuas

Day 1 (page 69)

physical characteristics: smallest breed of dog weighing 4 to 6 pounds (2 to 3 kilograms); can be long- or short-haired; life expectancy of 12 to 20 years; coats can be any color, either solid or multi-colored

breed history: clay pots with dogs resembling modern Chihuahuas were found in Mexico from 100 C.E.; named after a state in Mexico called Chihuahua; possibly descended from the Fennec fox, which is small with big eyes and ears

temperament and personality: considered a difficult breed to housebreak, or train; intelligent and loyal to its owner; like to burrow in pillows and blankets

Day 3 (page 71)

Newborn puppies are cute**, but** they need a lot of help during their first few weeks; They cannot even maintain their body temperature**, and** (or **so**) they huddle together to stay warm; After about two weeks, the puppies' sealed ears and eyes open**, and** at three weeks, they begin to walk.

Day 4 (page 72)

1. were eating
2. was thinking
3. is feeding
4. are gobbling
5. will be shopping
6. will be growing

Day 5 (page 73)

See Informative/Explanatory Rubric on page 203.

Week 13: Yosemite

Day 1 (page 74)

Beginning: gather hiking supplies at camp

Middle: climb to the top of the mountain and look out over land; see deer, fox, and bobcat while hiking; stop at a stream for water

End: walk back to camp

Day 2 (page 75)

1. Students may say that it is a strong draft because it includes a beginning, middle, and an end to a story. It also includes lots of adjectives.

Day 3 (page 76)

Answers may include:

1. gorgeous, breathtaking
2. huge, enormous
3. icy, freezing
4. exciting, eventful

Day 4 (page 77)

1. **"**The sequoia trees are so tall**,"** said the hiker.
2. The tour guide said**, "**Yosemite was started in 1890.**"**
3. **"**I've never seen anything so beautiful**,"** said the visitor.
4. Dad said**, "**It's time for bed because we are hiking tomorrow.**"**
5. **"**Let's come again next year**,"** said the son.

ANSWER KEY *(cont.)*

Week 14: Grand Canyon

Day 3 (page 81)

Example answers:

My adventurous family and I went rafting in the large, beautiful Grand Canyon.

Everyone was unbelievably scared except for me.

The wild, crashing water was rough.

One of the heaviest backpacks fell out of the thrashing raft.

Day 5 (page 83)

See Narrative Writing Rubric on page 204.

Week 15: Four Square

Day 1 (page 84)

Answers may include: I played on Wednesday when it was windy.; Marco kept catching the ball.; Meg kicked the ball by accident.; Marco argued about the ball hitting the line.; Lauren was alone, so we invited her to join us.; I never got out.

Day 2 (page 85)

Order may vary but could include:

2. Marco kept catching the ball, and we had to remind him to only hit it.
4. Once Meg got confused and kicked the ball, which was really funny.
1. A girl was standing by herself, not playing with anyone, so we invited her to join us.
3. Marco also argued with us about the ball hitting the line when he served.
5. The best part of playing was that I did not get out one time.

Day 3 (page 86)

1. A. entertaining
2. A. swat
3. C. changeable
4. B. gear
5. Answers will vary.

Day 4 (page 87)

1. whom
2. that
3. who
4. whose
5. which

Day 5 (page 88)

1. The paragraph is well organized and describes the events that happen.
2. The author could have used more adjectives to make the writing more exciting.

Week 16: Kickball

Day 3 (page 91)

Example answers:

Today's Weather: cold, windy, sunny; A Kickball: round, red, bouncy; Student: tall, freckled, strong

1. The strong student kicked the red kickball during the windy recess.
2. The round kickball sailed over the tall student's head.
3. The cold weather couldn't stop the freckled student from playing.

Day 4 (page 92)

that, which, whom, whom, whose

Day 5 (page 93)

See Narrative Writing Rubric on page 204.

Week 17: The Wright Brothers

Day 1 (page 94)

The first flight was on December 17, 1903, in Kitty Hawk, North Carolina; It was the first motor-powered flight with a person; Orville flew 120 feet (37 meters) in 12 seconds; The brothers chose Kitty Hawk, North Carolina, because of wind and soft sand; Both Orville and Wilbur flew later that day.

Day 2 (page 95)

1. Cross out: "When the French heard, they were skeptical the flight actually happened." This sentence should be left out because it is not about the first flight, which is the main idea of the paragraph.

Day 3 (page 96)

1. feet
2. children
3. people
4. geese
5. mice
6. women

Day 4 (page 97)

1. **The Wright Brothers** (capitalized because it is a proper noun) made history and accomplished a life-long dream.
2. **The** (capitalized because it is the first word in a sentence) historic flight happened on **December** (capitalized because it is the name of a month) 17, 1903, in **Kitty Hawk, North Carolina**. (capitalized because it is a proper noun)
3. **Orville** and **Wilbur** (capitalized because they are names of people) were from **Ohio** (capitalized because it is a proper noun), but went to **North Carolina** (capitalized because it is a proper noun) for the flight.

ANSWER KEY *(cont.)*

Week 18: Henry Ford

Day 1 (page 99)

It was made with interchangeable parts, so the car took less time to make; Workers were paid $5.00 a day; most other workers were paid $2.34 a day; It was made on a moving assembly line, so the car was less expensive to make; It was introduced in October 1908; It was nicknamed the "Tin Lizzie"

Day 3 (page 101)

lives, churches, beaches, wrenches, wives

Day 4 (page 102)

Capitalize: Model-T, Tin Lizzie, Model-T, Henry Ford, America, Tin Lizzie

Lowercase: popular, cars, black, steering wheel, auto world

Day 5 (page 103)

See Informative/Explanatory Writing Rubric on page 203.

Week 19: Snowboarding

Day 3 (page 106)

1. back to square one
2. costs an arm and a leg
3. best of both worlds.

Day 4 (page 107)

1. **"**That stuff is expensive**!"** she exclaimed**.**
2. Samuel asked**, "**Where is my snowboard**?"**
3. **"**This is awesome**!"** he yelled**.**
4. **"**May I borrow your goggles today**?"** Ella asked her brother**.**
5. **"**Most of all he wanted to do a flip**,"** Ella said**.**

Week 20: Ice Skating

Day 3 (page 111)

1. B. ring a bell
2. E. at the drop of a hat
3. A. cold shoulder
4. C. joined at the hip
5. D. split hairs

Day 4 (page 112)

1. "**Falling** down hurts!" exclaimed Jess.
2. "When are we leaving for the rink**?**" asked Edward**.**
3. Sierra said, "**Black** ice skates are my favorite."
4. Jeremiah asked**,** "Are we going to be late for practice?"
5. "I love gliding along the ice**,**" stated Rachael.

Day 5 (page 113)

See Narrative Writing Rubric on page 204.

Week 21: Mozart

Day 1 (page 114)

1. Y
2. N
3. N
4. N
5. Y
6. Y

Day 2 (page 115)

Possible sentences include: , it needed to be shared with others, people had to do what royalty said; He or his family could have suffered severe consequences.

Day 3 (page 116)

1. retry
2. mistreated
3. preview
4. rediscovered

Day 4 (page 117)

1. inside
2. on
3. into
4. across
5. toward
6. under
7. before
8. after

Day 5 (page 118)

1. The author could tell more about what consequences Mozart and his family would have faced had they refused.

Week 22: Beethoven

Day 3 (page 121)

1. **pre**dates
2. **pre**school
3. **un**fortunate
4. **re**visited
5. **mis**understood
6. Student answers will vary.

Day 4 (page 122)

in, of, near, to, through, on

Day 5 (page 123)

See Opinion Writing Rubric on page 202.

Week 23: Asteroids

Day 1 (page 124)

Billions or trillions of asteroids are in the asteroid belt; Sizes range from a pebble to over 150 miles (241 kilometers) in diameter; The dwarf planet Ceres is part of the asteroid belt; The asteroids are 600,000 miles (965,606 kilometers) apart; Most of the asteroids are lumpy.

Day 2 (page 125)

Underline: Small pebbles to 150 miles (241 kilometers) diameter; Asteroids 600,000 miles (965,606 kilometers) apart; Lumpy not round.

Day 3 (page 126)

1. **The dwarf planet Ceres** is an asteroid in the asteroid belt.
2. **Ceres** was discovered in 1801 by Giuseppe Piazzi.
3. **The asteroid** is about one-fourth the size of Earth's moon.
4. **The Herschel Space Observatory** discovered water vapor on Ceres.
5. **A year on Ceres** is equal to 4.6 Earth years.
6. Student answers will vary.

Day 4 (page 127)

1. definition 4
2. definition 3
3. Student answers will vary.

ANSWER KEY *(cont.)*

Week 24: Comets

Day 1 (page 129)

three parts: nucleus, coma, tail; nucleus: solid center made of dust and ice; coma: gas and dust atmosphere around nucleus; 2 tails: dust and plasma; look like "dirty snowballs"

Day 4 (page 132)

1. definition 2
2. definition 3
3. Student answers will vary.

Day 5 (page 133)

See Informative/Explanatory Writing Rubric on page 203.

Week 25: Solar Energy

Day 1 (page 134)

Advantages: does not produce pollution; once built, has low operating cost, is a clean, renewable resource, costs are coming down over time

Disadvantages: cannot collect energy at night or on cloudy days; expensive to install; not very efficient at changing energy to electricity

Day 2 (page 135)

Underline: Unlike traditional energy sources, solar energy does not produce any pollution; It is a clean, renewable resource, which means it will last without getting used up; Solar panels are expensive to install, but they're getting less expensive every year and users save a lot of money; Once the equipment has been built and installed, there is no operating cost because sunlight is free.

Day 3 (page 136)

1. C. there
2. A. They're
3. C. There
4. B. their

Day 4 (page 137)

1. Solar **energy** is hard for cloudy, rainy countries like **England**.
2. Heat and energy are two products of the **sun**.
3. Solar is the **Latin** word for sun.
4. In the 1830s, a man named **John Herschel** used solar energy to cook **food**.
5. The energy can be stored in **batteries** to use during the **night**.

Day 5 (page 138)

1. The author includes some reasons that do not support his or her opinion. To make it better, the author could have stated these reasons, but then explain why solar energy is still a good thing.

Week 26: Turbines

Day 1 (page 139)

Advantages: tall, but do not take up much land; wind is free; does not create pollution or greenhouse gases; good for remote areas without access to electricity.

Disadvantages: if it is not windy, no energy is created; noisy to nearby homes and businesses; nearly half a million birds are killed by turbine blades each year; clutter land, which some people say is ugly

Day 4 (page 142)

Capitalize: Persians, Middle East, Europeans, English, Dutch, United States, America

Lowercase: turbines, windmills, first, century, water, grain, windmills, energy

Day 5 (page 143)

See Opinion Writing Rubric on page 202.

Week 27: Mount Everest

Day 1 (page 144)

Yes: Being allowed to climb should be based on capability not age; If a child's parent allows it, the officials at Mount Everest should not interfere; Climbing promotes a healthy lifestyle, which could positively influence peers; No: It's dangerous because hundreds of people have died trying to reach the top; Teens' brains are not fully developed to make big decisions; Altitude sickness may affect young people differently than adults.

Day 2 (page 145)

Underline: Teens who climb are promoting healthy lifestyles, which could be positive influences on their peers; Reaching the summit would be very exciting for a young person; People of all ages should be allowed the thrill of experiencing the summit.

Day 3 (page 146)

1. B. dismiss
2. A. lose
3. B. poor
4. C. harmless
5. C. limited
6. A. small

Day 4 (page 147)

1. whom
2. who
3. who
4. whom
5. who

ANSWER KEY *(cont.)*

Week 28: Mount Kilimanjaro

Day 3 (page 151)

1. Mount Kilimanjaro is the **tallest** free-standing mountain, which means it is not part of a mountain range.
2. January through March are the **warmest** months in Tanzania.
3. The mountain's national park **opened** in 1977.
4. The **oldest** person to reach the summit was an 87-year-old Frenchman.
5. The **first** recorded summit of Mount Kilimanjaro was in 1889.

Day 4 (page 152)

1. C
2. I; **Who** is wearing the boots?
3. C
4. I; To **whom** will you give the pack?
5. C

Day 5 (page 153)

See Opinion Writing Rubric on page 202.

Week 29: Sculpture

Day 1 (page 154)

No cloudy or cracked ice is used; It can be made with a mold; Clear ice is made by shooting air into the water as it freezes; It can be made by hand using chainsaws, drills, and chisels; It is heated by a blowtorch at the end to make them shiny; It can be made by a rotating machine called a *lathe.*

Day 2 (page 155)

Underline: To make perfect ice, air jets are used to blow air into the water as it freezes; Sculptures can be made by hand, but artists typically use chainsaws and chisels to create them; Molds can also be used; A small blowtorch is used to make the sculpture shiny after the carving is complete; Machines called *lathes* can create sculptures quickly and efficiently.

Day 3 (page 156)

1. to decorate; for a special event
2. To make perfect ice; to blow air; into the water; as it freezes
3. by hand; to create them
4. to make the sculpture shiny; after the carving
5. Student answers will vary

Day 4 (page 157)

1. A. allowed
2. B. through
3. B. whether
4. A. mist
5. A. except
6. B. coarse

Day 5 (page 158)

1. The paragraph includes lots of information about ice scultpures and it could have explained more about how ice sculptures are imaginative forms of art.

Week 30: Painting

Day 1 (page 159)

bold color; paint dribbles or splashes; geometric shapes; no recognizable subject; open to interpretation

Day 4 (page 162)

1. knows
2. whole
3. wait
4. bare
5. flower
6. night
7. pail
8. meet

Day 5 (page 163)

See Informative/Explanatory Rubric on page 203.

Week 31: Steam Engine Trains

Day 1 (page 164)

Stars: The engines can be anywhere instead of being stuck by a river or a lake; One steam engine is equal to the power of many horses; Other energy sources, like wind, can only be used under the right weather conditions.

X's: The smoke puts air pollution into the environment; Boilers can burst, leading to loss of workers' lives and property.

Day 2 (page 165)

Most power before the 1800s required being close to water sources, but the steam engine train allowed distance from water; steam engine trains could work regardless of the environment; Horses were commonly used for travel, but a steam engine train was equal to the power of many horses.

Day 3 (page 166)

1. B. searching
2. B. lake
3. A. impossible
4. A. hills

Day 4 (page 167)

1. C; America's
2. I; train's
3. I; stations'
4. C; workers'

ANSWER KEY *(cont.)*

Week 32: Bullet Trains

Day 3 (page 171)

1. *Wandering* means the passenger didn't really have a purpose, but *walking* means he went right to the station.
2. *Glared* means she was looking at him with an angry expression, but *stared* means she looked at him for a long time.
3. *Tossing* is a gentle throw, but *hurling* is throwing something hard and often in anger.
4. An *argument* is fighting with anger, but a *disagreement* is discussing a difference of opinion in a gentler way.

Day 4 (page 172)

1. Japan's
2. bullet train's
3. Passengers'
4. system's
5. countries'

Day 5 (page 173)

See Opinion Writing Rubric on page 202.

Week 33: Eiffel Tower

Day 2 (page 175)

It was her last day in Paris, and she was finally going to see the Eiffel Tower; She climbed up all 1,665 steps to get to the top; As she looked over Paris, she saw clouds like cotton balls and a sunset striping the sky; She could see for miles; The sun slipped below the horizon and the lights on the Eiffel Tower turned on; This would definitely be her favorite memory of Paris.

Day 3 (page 176)

1. S; feels like butterflies are in her stomach
2. M; is a zoo
3. M; stripes the sky
4. S; clouds like cotton balls
5. S; as bright as the sun

Day 4 (page 177)

1. **The Eiffel Tower** was built in 1889.
2. It was built to be the **entrance arch** for the **World's Fair**.
3. The **tower** is repainted every seven years to protect it from **rust**.
4. There are 20,000 **lightbulbs** on the Eiffel **Tower**.
5. It was almost torn down but was kept because it could be used as a **radio antenna**.

Week 34: Leaning Tower of Pisa

Day 3 (page 181)

1. S; as an arrow
2. S; as a fishhook
3. M; light of Pisa
4. S; moths to a flame

Day 4 (page 182)

1. **During World War** II, the **Leaning Tower** of **Pisa** was almost destroyed.
2. **Many** tall buildings in **Italy** were being used as lookout towers by **Nazis**.
3. **American** soldiers were ordered to bomb any potential lookouts.
4. **The** beauty of the **Leaning Tower** of **Pisa** saved it from destruction.

Day 5 (page 183)

See Narrative Writing Rubric on page 204.

Week 35: Camping

Day 1 (page 184)

I was excited to go on my first camping trip; Everything seemed to go wrong; We couldn't get the tent set up; My mom forgot the cooler with the drinks; Dad worked for over an hour to start the fire; I dropped my hot dog into the fire; When we finally got settled, it started to rain.

Day 2 (page 185)

Underlined parts should include sentences that describe what is happening in the story.

Day 3 (page 186)

1. smooth**ly**
2. patient**ly**
3. Dark**ness**
4. hope**ful**
5. cloud**y**

Day 4 (page 187)

1. My dad said**, "**We can sleep under the beautiful sky.**"**
2. **"**I forgot the cooler at home**,"** she said.
3. **"**It's too cloudy**,"** my sister said to herself.

Week 36: Swimming

Day 3 (page 191)

1. A. enjoyable
2. A. weightless
3. B. careful
4. A. thankful

Day 4 (page 192)

1. **"**Can I go swim in the ocean?**"** the boy asked his mother.
2. **"**Not until I am ready to go with you**,"** his mother responded.
3. The boy stomped his foot and cried**, "**I want to go now!**"**
4. **"**It is not safe to go swimming alone**,"** his mother gently explained.
5. **"**I understand. Are you ready now?**"** he asked with a grin.

Day 5 (page 193)

See Narrative Writing Rubric on page 204.

OPINION WRITING RUBRIC

Directions: Evaluate students' work in each category by circling one number in each row. Students have opportunities to score up to five points in each row and up to 15 points total.

	Exceptional Writing		Quality Writing		Developing Writing	
Focus and Organization	Clearly states an opinion that is relevant to the topic. Demonstrates clear understanding of the intended audience and purpose of the piece. Organizes ideas in a purposeful way and includes an introduction, a detailed body, and a conclusion.		States an opinion that is relevant to the topic. Demonstrates some understanding of the intended audience and purpose of the piece. Organizes ideas and includes an introduction, a body, and a conclusion.		States an unclear opinion that is not fully relevant to the topic. Demonstrates little understanding of the intended audience or purpose of the piece. Does not include an introduction, a body, or a conclusion.	
Points	5	4	3	2	1	0
Written Expression	Uses descriptive and precise language with clarity and intention. Maintains a consistent voice and uses an appropriate tone that supports meaning. Uses multiple sentence types and transitions smoothly between ideas.		Uses a broad vocabulary. Maintains a consistent voice and supports a tone and feeling through language. Varies sentence length and word choices.		Uses a limited or an unvaried vocabulary. Provides an inconsistent or a weak voice and tone. Provides little to no variation in sentence type and length.	
Points	5	4	3	2	1	0
Language Conventions	Capitalizes, punctuates, and spells accurately. Demonstrates complete thoughts within sentences, with accurate subject-verb agreement. Uses paragraphs appropriately and with clear purpose.		Capitalizes, punctuates, and spells accurately. Demonstrates complete thoughts within sentences and appropriate grammar. Paragraphs are properly divided and supported.		Incorrectly capitalizes, punctuates, and spells. Uses fragmented or run-on sentences. Utilizes poor grammar overall. Paragraphs are poorly divided and developed.	
Points	5	4	3	2	1	0

Total Points: ____________________

INFORMATIVE/EXPLANATORY WRITING RUBRIC

Directions: Evaluate students' work in each category by circling one number in each row. Students have opportunities to score up to five points in each row and up to 15 points total.

	Exceptional Writing		Quality Writing		Developing Writing	
Focus and Organization	Clearly states the topic and purposefully develops it throughout the writing. Demonstrates clear understanding of the intended audience and purpose of the piece. Organizes the information into a well-supported introduction, body, and conclusion.		States the topic and develops it throughout the writing. Demonstrates some understanding of the intended audience and purpose of the piece. Organizes the information into an introduction, body, and conclusion.		Does not state the topic and/or develop it throughout the writing. Demonstrates little understanding of the intended audience or purpose of the piece. Fails to organize the information into an introduction, body, or conclusion.	
Points	5	4	3	2	1	0
Written Expression	Uses descriptive and precise language with clarity and intention. Maintains a consistent voice and uses an appropriate tone that supports meaning. Uses multiple sentence types and transitions smoothly between ideas.		Uses a broad vocabulary. Maintains a consistent voice and supports a tone and feeling through language. Varies sentence length and word choices.		Uses a limited or an unvaried vocabulary. Provides an inconsistent or a weak voice and tone. Provides little to no variation in sentence type and length.	
Points	5	4	3	2	1	0
Language Conventions	Capitalizes, punctuates, and spells accurately. Demonstrates complete thoughts within sentences, with accurate subject-verb agreement. Uses paragraphs appropriately and with clear purpose.		Capitalizes, punctuates, and spells accurately. Demonstrates complete thoughts within sentences and appropriate grammar. Paragraphs are properly divided and supported.		Incorrectly capitalizes, punctuates, and spells. Uses fragmented or run-on sentences. Utilizes poor grammar overall. Paragraphs are poorly divided and developed.	
Points	5	4	3	2	1	0

Total Points: ____________________

NARRATIVE WRITING RUBRIC

Directions: Evaluate students' work in each category by circling one number in each row. Students have opportunities to score up to five points in each row and up to 15 points total.

	Exceptional Writing		**Quality Writing**		**Developing Writing**	
Focus and Organization	Identifies the topic of the story and maintains the focus throughout the writing. Develops clear settings, a strong plot, and interesting characters. Demonstrates clear understanding of the intended audience and purpose of the piece. Engages the reader from the opening hook through the middle to the conclusion.		Identifies the topic of the story, but has some trouble maintaining the focus throughout the writing. Develops settings, a plot, and characters. Demonstrates some understanding of the intended audience and purpose of the piece. Includes an interesting opening, a strong story, and a conclusion.		Fails to identify the topic of the story or maintain focus throughout the writing. Does not develop strong settings, plot, or characters. Demonstrates little understanding of the intended audience or purpose of the piece. Provides lack of clarity in the beginning, middle, and/or conclusion.	
Points	5	4	3	2	1	0
Written Expression	Uses descriptive and precise language with clarity and intention. Maintains a consistent voice and uses an appropriate tone that supports meaning. Uses multiple sentence types and transitions smoothly between ideas.		Uses a broad vocabulary. Maintains a consistent voice and supports a tone and feeling through language. Varies sentence length and word choices.		Uses a limited or an unvaried vocabulary. Provides an inconsistent or a weak voice and tone. Provides little to no variation in sentence type and length.	
Points	5	4	3	2	1	0
Language Conventions	Capitalizes, punctuates, and spells accurately. Demonstrates complete thoughts within sentences, with accurate subject-verb agreement. Uses paragraphs appropriately and with clear purpose.		Capitalizes, punctuates, and spells accurately. Demonstrates complete thoughts within sentences and appropriate grammar. Paragraphs are properly divided and supported.		Incorrectly capitalizes, punctuates, and spells. Uses fragmented or run-on sentences. Utilizes poor grammar overall. Paragraphs are poorly divided and developed.	
Points	5	4	3	2	1	0

Total Points: ____________________

OPINION WRITING ANALYSIS

Directions: Record each student's rubric scores (page 202) in the appropriate columns. Add the totals every two weeks and record the sums in the Total Scores column. You can view: (1) which students are not understanding the opinion genre and (2) how students progress after multiple encounters with the opinion genre.

	Week 4	Week 10	Week 22	Week 26	Week 28	Week 32	Total Scores
Student Name							
Average Classroom Score							

INFORMATIVE/EXPLANATORY WRITING ANALYSIS

Directions: Record each student's rubric score (page 203) in the appropriate columns. Add the totals every two weeks and record the sums in the Total Scores column. You can view: (1) which students are not understanding the informative/explanatory genre and (2) how students progress after multiple encounters with the informative/explanatory genre.

	Week 2	**Week 8**	**Week 12**	**Week 18**	**Week 24**	**Week 30**	**Total Scores**
Student Name							
Average Classroom Score							

NARRATIVE WRITING ANALYSIS

Directions: Record each student's rubric score (page 204) in the appropriate columns. Add the totals every two weeks and record the sums in the Total Scores column. You can view: (1) which students are not understanding the narrative genre and (2) how students progress after multiple encounters with the narrative genre.

	Week 6	Week 14	Week 16	Week 20	Week 34	Week 36	Total Scores
Student Name							
Average Classroom Score							

THE WRITING PROCESS

STEP 1: PREWRITING

Think about the topic. Brainstorm ideas, and plan what you want to include in your writing.

STEP 2: DRAFTING

Use your brainstormed ideas to write a first draft. Don't worry about errors. This will be a rough draft.

STEP 3: REVISING

Read your rough draft. Think about the vocabulary you used and how your writing is organized. Then, make the appropriate changes to improve your written piece.

STEP 4: EDITING

Reread your revised draft. Check for errors in spelling, punctuation, and grammar. Use editing marks to correct the errors.

STEP 5: PUBLISHING

Create a final version of your piece, including the corrections from the edited version. Be sure to reread your work for any errors.

EDITING MARKS

Editing Marks	Symbol Names	Example
≡	capitalization symbol	david gobbled up the grapes.
/	lowercase symbol	My mother hugged Me when I Came Home.
⊙	insert period symbol	The clouds danced in the sky .
sp ○	check spelling symbol	sp I laffed at the story.
∽	transpose symbol	How you are?
^	insert symbol	Would you please pass the pizza?
^ ,	insert comma symbol	I have two cats, two dogs, and a goldfish.
“ ”	insert quotations symbol	“That's amazing,” she shouted.
ℓ	deletion symbol	Will you call call me on the phone tonight?
¶	new paragraph symbol	... in the tree. ¶ After lunch, I spent the day...
#	add space symbol	I ran tothe tree.

OPINION WRITING TIPS

Ask yourself . . .	Remember . . .
Do I have a strong belief in my opinion so that I can convince others to believe the same?	Make sure you can back up your opinion with specific examples.
Have I stated my opinion in a way that grabs the reader's attention?	Begin with a question or a bold statement that includes your opinion.
Do I have at least three reasons based on facts for my opinion?	Include at least three solid reasons why the reader should agree with you.
Do I have an example for each reason that strengthens my argument?	Each reason must be followed by one strong example.
Do I have a logical order to my writing?	Don't bounce around. Focus on a logical order to present each reason and example.
Am I using smooth transitions to connect my thoughts and help my writing flow?	Use transition words like *first*, *in addition to*, *another reason*, and *most important*.
Does my conclusion restate my opinion?	Do not forget to restate your opinion in the final sentence.
Have I used correct spelling, grammar, and punctuation?	Revisit what you have written. Then, check for mistakes.

INFORMATIVE/EXPLANATORY WRITING TIPS

Ask yourself . . .	Remember . . .
Do I provide enough information on the topic?	Make sure to include facts about the topic in your writing so that the reader is informed.
Have I narrowed the focus of the topic?	Choose one aspect of the topic that you want to write about.
Does my writing have a hook?	Begin with a strong topic sentence that grabs the reader's attention.
Is my information presented in a logical order?	Do not bounce around. Present each topic sentence at the beginning of a paragraph and add details.
Have I included enough information that the reader will be interested in learning even more?	End with a strong sentence that makes the reader want to learn more about the subject.
Have I used correct spelling, grammar, and punctuation?	Revisit what you have written. Then, check for mistakes.

NARRATIVE WRITING TIPS

Ask yourself . . .	Remember . . .
Am I the main character? Is the story told from my point of view?	You are in the story, telling where you are, what you see, who you are with, and what you do.
Does my story have a hook?	Include an exciting introductory sentence that makes the reader want to continue reading.
Does my story make sense and have a beginning, a middle, and an end?	Do not bounce around. Focus on a logical order of how the experience happened.
Am I using transitions to connect my thoughts and help the writing flow?	Use transition words like *first*, *next*, *then*, *another*, and *finally*.
Am I including rich details and sensory language to help paint a picture in the reader's mind?	Use lots of adjectives, and incorporate figurative language, such as metaphors and similes, to make your story come to life.
Does my conclusion summarize the main idea?	Incorporate a sentence or two that reflects on what you have written.
Have I used correct spelling, grammar, and punctuation?	Revisit what you have written. Then, check for mistakes.

Opinion Writing

Informative/Explanatory Writing

Narrative Writing

DIGITAL RESOURCES

Accessing the Digital Resources

The digital resources can be downloaded by following these steps:

1. Go to **www.tcmpub.com/digital**
2. Sign in or create an account.
3. Click **Redeem Content** and enter the ISBN number, located on page 2 and the back cover, into the appropriate field on the website.
4. Respond to the prompts using the book to view your account and available digital content.
5. Choose the digital resources you would like to download. You can download all the files at once, or you can download a specific group of files.

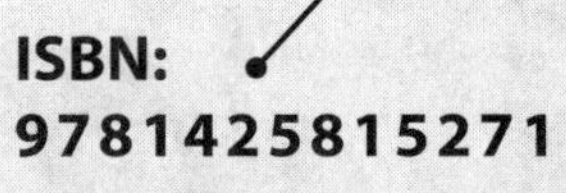

Please note: Some files provided for download have large file sizes. Download times for these larger files will vary based on your download speed.

CONTENTS OF THE DIGITAL RESOURCES

Teacher Resources

- Informative/Explanatory Writing Analysis
- Narrative Writing Analysis
- Opinion Writing Analysis
- Writing Rubric
- Writing Signs

Student Resources

- Peer/Self-Editing Checklist
- Editing Marks
- Practice Pages
- The Writing Process
- Writing Prompts
- Writing Tips

